Pierre Eade speaks with wisdom and clarity. This book is concise, yet full of deep insight. Pierre uses metaphors, illustrations, and stories seamlessly to articulate each point. Each chapter ends with questions & meditations, making this a great resource for individuals as well as small groups. Whether you have been a Christian for years, have just started your journey with Christ, or are not quite sure what you believe, this book is for you; it will make you laugh, encourage you, and help you to grow in your understanding of God the Father.

NICK AGAZARIAN, YOUTH PASTOR

I love the premise of this book: Let Jesus, who knows Him best, tell you what the Father is like. After all, He can reveal the Father like no one else. Written in a down to earth, easy to read, and well-illustrated style, this book will help you to appreciate afresh our Good Father. If you are a man with a father wound, this book will help you find healing in the Father's love.

DAVE ARMSTRONG, MAN IN THE MIRROR, AREA DIRECTOR

The experiences we have with our earthly fathers deeply inform our understanding of our Heavenly Father. Pierre Eade bridges the gap for a generation of Americans that seem to be distant from both. Like a conversation with an old friend, *Our Good Father* is an essential guide that reintroduces God the Father with comfort and clarity. We can all learn from this book.

TOM EBERSOLE, SENIOR PASTOR, WAYNE UMC

I read few books that I find so beneficial not only to myself but also to fellow Christians as well as unchurched friends. I really appreciated the premise of getting to know our Heavenly Father through His Son. This book addressed the topic of the father wound with sensitivity and points us to our Heavenly Father as a perfect Father. We are reminded that we no longer need to be defined by our earthly father but, as God's children, we are now defined by Our Good Father who loves and accepts us unconditionally. This is a message we all need to hear. I personally appreciate that Pierre has given us a great resource in assisting us in the pursuit of our most important relationship. I also love the epilogue which encourages additional study.

JOEL W. FISCUS, VP OF FIELD STAFF AND MINISTRY TO MEN,
CHRISTIAN SERVICE BRIGADES MINISTRIES

What a beautiful and refreshing portrait of God the Father. This insightful, easy-to-read and biblical book will capture—or re-capture— your faith in His extravagant love for you.

CHRIS FRANCIS, PASTOR OF TRUE LIFE CHURCH

Our Good Father will help anyone strengthen their relationship and understand their relationship with God better on their own personal spiritual journey. There are heartfelt personal stories that will help anyone connect much closer to God. This book also brings up questions that we should all be asking ourselves about our relationship with God.

DR. KEVIN KITA, CHIROPRACTOR, SPEAKER, AUTHOR OF *HEALING JOURNEYS*

Pierre Eade has the capacity to take the complicated and convoluted and express in simple yet profound words. *Our Good Father* helps unveil the love of God seen through the eyes of Jesus. Pierre's writing will awaken your imagination and stir your soul. Be aware his observations of Good Father could cut right through old baggage and misperceptions.

PHILIP MCVAY, LEAD PASTOR, SHALIMAR UMC

Pierre takes a closer look at what ails all of our aching hearts. Our first source of love comes from our parents. Many of us have been hurt and pained by our earthly father and transfer these hurt feelings onto God never giving God a chance to prove himself. Pierre takes one on a journey from our disappointed father experience to an exquisite relationship with a perfect father who loves, provides and protects us.

ESTHER MILLS, MA, LAC, BSC, CHRISTIAN COUNSELOR

Pierre does an excellent job of bringing the reader on a journey of discovery alongside with him, in his new book *Our Good Father*. Discovering the truth of who God our Father is as revealed to us by Jesus Christ is one of the most important teachings in the Bible, and Pierre does an amazing job of explaining profound truths in a simple and understandable way. God's heart is revealed in this book, a must read!

CHRIS MIRRLEES , LEAD PASTOR, AUTHOR OF
THE BALANCED APPROACH TO HEALING

An astonishingly great book by an amazing emerging writer, *Our Good Father* by Pierre Eade grips the reader with personal bare-your-soul illustrations and applications and embraces the reader with the wonderful reality and presence of our gracious and wonderful Father God. Especially helpful are the group discussions following each chapter that makes this an excellent study for small groups and classes. As an educator, I grade this book a 100 out of 100!

DR. LEE SIMMONS, INTERNATIONAL DIRECTOR, MISSIO GLOBAL MINISTRIES

Like Pierre, I grew up in church and knew God as Savior, but not as Father. With so many poor examples of fathers in our world today, this can be a difficult concept to grasp, but those who do will be forever changed. I love the way *Our Good Father* blends Scripture, rich theology, and personal stories into a highly readable text. Join Pierre as he takes you on a journey into the father heart of God.

JARED STUMP, FOUNDER OF LIVING FROM THE HEART MINISTRIES; AUTHOR OF *CREATION & REDEMPTION: FINDING YOUR PLACE IN A FALLEN WORLD*

OUR GOOD
FATHER

OUR GOOD FATHER

PIERRE M. EADE

BRIDGE
LOGOS

Newberry, FL 32669

Bridge-Logos
Newberry, FL 32669, USA

Our Good Father:
Seeing God Through the Eyes of Jesus
Pierre Eade

Printed in the United States of America

Library of Congress Catalog Card Number: 2016961564

International Standard Book Number: 978-1-61036-177-4

BP VP 06-15-17

DEDICATION

The authors of the books we now call the Bible originally wrote with a specific audience in mind. Yet the words and message of the Holy Scriptures have been used by God to carry his message of love and redemption well beyond the original, contemporary readers in a way that has now blessed countless people and generations.

This book was created for you to read and enjoy with the hope of you coming to more fully know and experience the truth of God's goodness. Furthermore, in the heart of this author, is the desire to not only have this message be read today, but someday read by my own future generations to come.

So I dedicate this book to the future grandchildren, great grandchildren and beyond who I have not yet met or seen. My hope, heart and prayer for each of you is that you come to know the pure goodness of God our Father. No matter what people tell you or what life circumstances seem to indicate, always remember and trust that Our Father is good!

"I remain confident of this: I will see the goodness of the Lord in the land of the living" (Psalm 27:13)

ACKNOWLEDGEMENTS

First and foremost, I need to thank the dynamic trio – God the Father, Son and Holy Spirit. To my Father, thank you for loving me even beyond what the words of this book are able to articulate. Jesus, thank you for making it possible to know the goodness of our Father by revealing Him to us. Holy Spirit, as always, thanks for the inspiration!

I need to thank the people who attended the original Bible study that formed the basis for this book. Coming back each week was a compelling reason for me to keep working on this project! Thank you for your encouraging words along the way.

I want to thank Steve Myers, one of the godliest men I have ever known. Steve, thank you for reading through every rough draft and providing biblically accurate, Holy Spirit sensitive advice and counsel. I am truly grateful for your love, example, service and friendship.

A special thanks to Jeanette Windle who after reading through the manuscript advised me not to rush the publication of this book because she believed God wanted it to reach a much broader audience. I felt the gentle yet firm nudge of the Holy Spirit through you, Jeanette. Thank you for your encouragement and wise counsel.

Last, but by no means least, I want to thank the team of people who faithfully prayed for this book's success. My prayer is that Our Good Father will reward you greatly in return.

TABLE OF CONTENTS

Before You Dive In

Every journey has a beginning. At times, we feel well equipped to begin the journey before us and other times we feel unprepared. It's the difference between receiving swimming lessons from a certified swim instructor versus an older sibling who decides to throw you into the deep end of the pool. As you journey into the discovery of Our Good Father, I want you to be well prepared so you can swim as deep as possible in the waters of this book. At the end of each chapter, you will find several study guides that will help you to do just that. Here is what you will find and how it is meant to help you navigate the waters.

Points to Remember

The points to remember are highlights from the chapter that help summarize the main message. These are the foundational truths, the pillars if you will, needed to establish your faith in Our Good Father.

Prayer

A prayer has been crafted to help connect the information you are learning to your relationship with God. Use these prayers as a jumpstart to your time with the Father. He is waiting to hear your voice.

Meditation

The meditation is a short sentence that is written primarily in the first person for the purpose of contemplation. Consider taking the meditation and reading it over slowly. You may want to close your eyes, practice deep breathing or just think on the words repeating them over and over again in your heart.

Group Discussion

Want to find the greatest benefit from reading this book? Gather together with a group of friends, family members, church members or co-workers and read one chapter at a time. Then, come together with your group to discuss the chapter, answer the questions and pray for one another. You will find that your journey together with others will take you so much deeper than you could ever reach on your own.

Dig Deeper

Passages of the Bible that were used during the chapter, and at times some additional passages, are listed here for your benefit. Look these verses up, read them in context and study them for yourself to dig deeper into the topic. If you're reading this book with a group, you can collectively study these verses.

Want More?

For additional resources to use in a group setting or teaching others please visit: www.ourgoodfather.com

Enjoy the Journey!

INTRODUCTION

A BLANK CANVAS

"A blank canvas…has unlimited possibilities."

— STEPHANIE PERKINS

One of my favorite childhood TV shows in the 1980s was *The Joy of Painting* hosted by a guy named Bob Ross. Bob was an amazing painter who knew how to transform a blank canvas into a masterpiece of "happy" little trees, mountains, skies, lakes, and forests in under 30 minutes.

Three things impressed me about Bob Ross apart from his magnificent paintings. The first was Bob's soft spoken nature. He could have put a whiney baby to sleep with his calming voice. Surprisingly, Bob Ross spent twenty years in the Air Force and retired with a rank of master sergeant. When he retired, he vowed never to scream again.[1] Go Bob!

The second incredible thing about Bob Ross was that he was a skinny guy with huge hair. I find skinny people to be cool. I also find big hair to be fun. Yet the combination of a skinny body with overgrown hair is straight up spectacular! Bob Ross's thin body and big hair

---

1   Shrieves, Linda. "Bob Ross Uses His Brush To Spread Paint And Joy" Orlando Sentinel. July 7, 1990. http://articles.orlandosentinel.com/1990-07-07/lifestyle/9007060122_1_bob-ross-joy-of-painting-pbs, accessed June 2, 2017.

combo made him look like a piece of broccoli. You just have to love skinny people with big hair!

The third amazing thing about Bob Ross was not the final product he painted, which was always beautiful. It was how midway through his painting he always seemed to completely ruin the picture. I'd be watching him paint, thinking it was going just fine and that we were about to witness another masterpiece unfold, when "Bam!" Bob Ross would slap on a blob of paint I was certain would wreck the whole deal. I'd think, "Bob, what in the world are you doing?" But in the end, Bob would again prove his brilliance (and coolness) by turning the painting into something serene and pristine. Good ol' Bob Ross.

My hope is that this book will paint a beautiful and irresistible picture of God the Father that you will love even more than I loved Bob Ross's paintings. But before we make a masterpiece, I want to stop and simply recognize that there may be a whole bunch of blotches and spots on your canvas, images of God the Father that have not yet been transformed into happy little trees, mountains and valleys.

FAMILY & RELIGIOUS BAGGAGE

Just calling God by the title of "Father" may be quite difficult for you. You may have an immediate internal reaction within your heart and mind because you superimpose a picture of your own dad on top of the painting of God the Father. You think to yourself, "My father was *too* busy for me." Or "My dad was *abusive*." Or "My dad was always *angry*." Or "My father was *religious, yet not loving*." Or "My dad was *absent*." Or "My dad was *uninvolved*." Or "My old man was an *alcoholic*." Or "My father was *non-existent*." And with more than a little attitude you protest, "You want me to call God 'Our Good Father'? No chance, buddy!"

We get stuck before the word go and especially before the word *good*. We have blotches of paint smeared all over our canvas, and the future of this painting does not look promising. How can we draw close to God the Father when the image we have from the onset is tainted by our workaholic, abusive, angry, religious yet unloving, absent, alcoholic, uninvolved, or simply never present biological fathers?

The first time I ever made the connection between the impact of our parents and especially our fathers have on our relationship with God was at a Christian conference. The speaker asked the group of men gathered together for a breakout session to yell out the impressions they had of their dads. From the front of the room you could hear men cheering things like, "Awesome!" "Loving!" "Strong!" And from the back of the room there were shouts in anger like, "Jerk!" "Loser!" and some other expletive words that I probably should not include in a Christian book.

What astonished me more than the stark contrast of expressions made by the men as well as the vigor in both tones was that I noticed how the men who apparently had good fathers chose the seats in the front of the room, whereas the men who had bad dads were heard from the back of the room. It was the first time that I ever made a real connection between the relationships we have with our biological fathers and how we view life. I made a mental note of this observation.

What can make this painting even messier is our religious upbringing. Many of us may view God as an angry, distant, and uncaring "man upstairs" who is out to get us. We may go to church a couple times a year or even every week, but to think of God as a Good Father or even a good friend is incomprehensible. Our various religious upbringings may have trained us to see God as a distant, cold, and unapproachable taskmaster who wants us to be quiet and sit up straight anytime we are in his house.

Or maybe you approach this topic differently. Your father was a decent man. He provided for your family. He coached your Little League baseball team or made it to every one of your dance recitals. Generally speaking, he did a good job. He wasn't perfect by any means, but he wasn't abusive either. And maybe your religious upbringing was for the most part positive. You were taught that God was benevolent and kind, patient and full of love. Let me assure you, in either extreme from bad to great, no father is quite like God the Father.

MY UPBRINGING

My own father, Elias Eade Jr., influenced my perceptions about God. My dad's grandmother emigrated to America from Lebanon with her two sons. Her husband, my great grandfather, never made it over to

The New World, for reasons unknown to this day. That meant the responsibility of providing for and raising her two sons in a new country fell completely into her lap. She was an entrepreneur, going from town to town selling various goods. My dad's father and his brother were raised under the tutelage of this strong, hardworking woman.

My dad's father Elias married a woman by the name of Yasmine who died at a young age. In the tradition of the time, when a man lost his wife, he would marry the next youngest daughter in the family. He married my grandmother Domina. My dad's father Elias and mother Domina worked hard to support their family and make it through the Great Depression.

My dad was drafted into the Army during the Korean War when he was twenty. He returned home from the Army two years later when his father suddenly passed away. My dad began working alongside his mother in running the family business. He inherited his parents' hard work ethic and his grandmother's entrepreneurial spirit and eventually ran his own business to support our family of six kids, of whom I am the youngest.

In many ways my dad painted a positive image of God in my mind—a strong, responsible, faithful, hardworking, sacrificial, morally upright provider who was committed to lead his family. As a child, I knew my dad loved me, not necessarily by showing me overwhelming affection (that came from my mom), but by his hard work to provide for our family.

Overall, I am very grateful for my dad and his influence in my life. I honor my father for what he has done to provide for six kids and give us a solid moral and spiritual compass to direct our lives. Thank you, Dad! I love you!

My view of God was no doubt impacted by my relationship with my father. I saw God as a good provider, one who gave strength and shelter and who wanted what was best for his children and was willing to sacrifice for it. My dad was not overly interactive and was definitely not the touchy-feely type. He would hug me and occasionally rub his scrubby beard against my soft kid face (something I loved), but he was not the type of dad who would go outside to play ball or wrestle with me.

In many ways, what my dad did not provide was made up by my older brother Paul. Paul was the one who signed me up for sports—including football against my mom's better judgment. Paul was the chummy older brother who would wrestle with me (never letting me win of course) and give me the physical love and affection every boy wants from a male role model. I learned vicariously through Paul what it meant to have a close, healthy bond with an older male authority figure.

My own understanding of God was also shaped by my religious upbringing. I was raised Maronite Catholic, what I consider the Lebanese flavor of Catholicism. We had the same basic beliefs as Roman Catholics, but our mass would include some special nuances such as saying certain prayers in Arabic and the burning of incense. I built up a serious tolerance for the smoke! My parents brought us to church faithfully every Sunday. I felt a true sense of community and belonging when in church and among the other Lebanese families from our small town of Olean, New York.

My catechism gave me an understanding of God as a powerful force not to be reckoned with or questioned. I memorized the top ten things God did *not* want me to do, but struggled to obey his hard and fast rules. I recognized God's authority and power, but never understood the friendship, relationship and intimacy he offered his children. The positive of this teaching was that I understood quite well the fear of the Lord. The major downside was that I never got the core message of God's love for me. God was someone to please, appease and obey. He was someone to be taken seriously, but not someone you really wanted to hang out with after church was over. So I tended not to think too much about him once Sunday mass and catechism ended.

COMING TO CHRIST

At the age of twenty-two, I accepted Jesus Christ as my Lord and Savior. After my conversion, Jesus became my best friend and brother, but the Father was still more like a distant being off in another galaxy. I kept my distance from him primarily out of fear, but also because I wasn't sure he really wanted anything to do with me. I figured that he sent my big brother Jesus to be his delegate to play and interact with his kids while he took care of other business, like managing the cosmos.

The Lord has blessed my wife Amanda and me with three healthy children who give us both great joy. In many ways, I see how the influence of the men in my own life has shaped my parenting and role as a dad. I can see how my dad's influence of strength, provision and leadership has shaped me as a father, husband and provider for my family. At the same time, my brother Paul's chumminess and playfulness has helped me be an interactive dad with my own kids.

When I became a father, my relationship with God the Father began to change. The birth of our children also gave birth to a desire within me to know God the Father more intimately. My innate love for my own children began to erode my previous concepts of a far, distant, and emotionless God. I began to realize that God the Father has a heart of love and grace for his children that far surpasses his kids' understanding. I started to see myself relating more and more to the heart of the Father.

I had spent twelve years working in corporate America when God opened up the door for me to serve in full-time ministry. At the writing of this book, I have served seven years as a pastor in our church where I oversee our local and global outreach, men's ministry and small groups. During my tenure as a pastor, I have witnessed firsthand how a person's upbringing and relationship to their parents affects not only their view of God, but their self-image, career choices, parenting, marriages and other important relationships.

I have also been amazed by the incredible power of praying for people to receive the Father's love and how good teaching on the Father heart of God never seems to lose its effectiveness, relevance or power. People really want to know what Father God is like, how he sees them, and if they are safe or welcomed to open their hearts and lives to him.

> *I AM EXCITED TO SHARE WHAT I FOUND BECAUSE I BELIEVE IT HAS THE POWER TO POSITIVELY IMPACT YOUR RELATIONSHIP WITH GOD THE FATHER AS IT DID FOR ME.*

In recent years, as I have contemplated the nature of God the Father, a question has come to mind that I could not dismiss. **How would Jesus describe the nature of his Father?** I began to wonder what would happen if I studied Christ's words about his Father to better understand his perspective. What began as a Bible study for my own personal growth and edification turned into the book that you now hold. I am excited to share what I found because I believe it has the power to positively impact your relationship with God the Father as it did for me.

PRESUPPOSITIONS

You see, whether we recognize it or not, we all approach the topic of God the Father with a load of presuppositions. A presupposition is an assumption or idea that we have in advance or take for granted.[2] It is a notion we carry around subconsciously about any aspect of life. It's our own prejudice based on past experience, knowledge, mindsets, our upbringing, culture, education, and every other imaginable idea that has been planted and cultivated in our minds from day one.

In their book *America's Four Gods*, Paul Froese and Christopher Bader, both Baylor University professors, explain the four contrasting ways Americans view God. Froese and Bader write, "While Americans almost universally view God as a loving parent, they are divided on whether God is best described as a firm or indulgent parent. And whether God is strict or forgiving proves an important distinction."[3] According to the authors, the level of engagement God has with humanity as well as the degree to which God is judgmental or forbearing put Americans into one of four main categories.

The first group sees God as an authoritarian who is "engaged in the world and judgmental".[4] The Authoritarian God is out to set the world straight. According to Froese and Bader's research, 31% of Americans view God in this light.

The second most typical view is that of a Distant God who in complete contrast to an Authoritarian God is disengaged and non-judgmental. The Distant God is one who does not really care or involve himself in human or world affairs. 24% of Americans view God this way. Equally popular among Americans (24%) is the view of God as

2   http://dictionary.reference.com/browse/presuppose
3   Froese, Paul. America's Four Gods: What We Say about God—and What That Says about Us (Kindle Locations 313-315). Oxford University Press. Kindle Edition.
4   Ibid. (Kindle Locations 437-438).

benevolent, someone who is loving, supportive, caring and actively involved in our lives.

Sixteen percent of Americans view God as being critical. He will judge us, but he's waiting for eternity to do so. For now, we're on our own. The remaining 5% do not believe God exists at all.[5]

The way in which each of us responds to life's tragedies, trials and struggles depends greatly upon our view of God. For example, if

> *OUR EVERYDAY LIFE, RELATIONSHIPS AND CHOICES ARE BEING AFFECTED BY OUR PERSONAL VIEW OF GOD.*

we view God as being distant and far removed, we are less likely to talk to him when times are tough than if we see him as benevolent and caring. Furthermore, our view of God will also affect our understanding of personal morality, politics, science, money, evil, war, and natural disasters. [6]

But the most important question still remains: Which view of God is the most accurate? Is God out to get us or to bless us? Is he far removed or right by our side?

Do not minimize the importance of this question! Our everyday life, relationships and choices are being affected by our personal view of God. Even an atheist makes life choices based on their belief about God or lack thereof. How we view God the Father is important for our life here and now as well as for eternity.

A BLANK CANVAS

I would like to challenge you at the start of this book to do something radical. It won't cost you a dime, but it could end up being the most priceless gift you have ever been given.

It is simply this: **Give God a blank canvas.**

"What do you mean by a blank canvas?" you ask. Good question. What I mean is simply this. When I say "God the Father", you picture

---

5 Americans' views of God shape attitudes on key issues, http://usatoday30.usatoday. com/news/religion/2010-10-07-1Agod07_CV_N.htm, accessed July 24, 2015.

6 Americans' views of God shape attitudes on key issues, http://usatoday30. usatoday.com/news/religion/2010-10-07-1Agod07_CV_N.htm, accessed July 24, 2015.

in your mind a blank canvas-nothing good, nothing bad, nothing at all, just blank. Now that's not too hard is it?

Now once you have a blank canvas in your mind, let me explain what we're going to do with it. We are going to ask Jesus to come and paint a picture of God the Father in your mind. It will be a whole new painting. It won't have any of the stains of the past or even of the present. It will be a completely new picture just for you.

"How will Jesus do that?" you ask. I have to say, you are asking all the right questions. Here is how he's going to do it. Jesus spoke a lot about God the Father. In fact, his Father was one of his top two favorite topics of all time to discuss, the other being the kingdom of God. Jesus spoke of God his Father as someone he knew quite personally and intimately, not just as one speaking out of theory or theology.

So for the remainder of this book, we are going to look into the words of Jesus concerning God the Father. We will in essence allow Jesus to paint the picture for us. And when Jesus paints a picture, it always turns out to be a masterpiece! *purpose of this book*

MY OWN LITTLE WORK OF ART

As Jesus is painting this picture, I will be coming alongside you to describe the significance of his words as best I possibly can. Consider me like a guide in a beautiful museum of pictures that Jesus has painted of Our Good Father. Each chapter is like a new painting.

Several months back I went to breakfast with my neighbor Larry, who is also a son of Our Good Father. As we were walking back home, he said to me with a real sense of awe and wonder, "Pierre, we cannot even begin to comprehend the goodness of Our Father." At that very moment, a picture came into my mind.

It was a painting that a child proudly made of their father. It was no Van Gogh, Kinkade or Ross painting by any stretch of the imagination. It looked more like a finger painting. The painting was a picture of the child artist's father. And with this image, came a beautiful and glorious thought that still captures my heart to this day.

We will never fully be able to grasp, comprehend or describe the goodness of God our Father this side of eternity. However, when we speak of his goodness and his love and make an attempt to describe his wonder, it is like a proud dad who sees the rudimentary painting of his child. He looks on it with joy and gladness and says to the child, "What a great job you have done!" With that said, I invite you to enjoy reading my humble, yet heartfelt portrayal of Our Good Father.

CHAPTER ONE

Jesus, the Master Painter

"Painting is just another way of keeping a diary."

— PABLO PICASSO

Over the years I have read through and studied the words of Jesus. As I focused on how he describes God the Father, I found that Jesus is trying to get across one clear message to us all: My Father is good!

That's it. Nothing too crazy. Nothing earth shattering. It is just a simple statement about his Father that he is altogether good. Now that would not be too hard a pill to swallow if it weren't for all the religious dogma our minds may have been chewing on for years. "God is angry." "God is out to get me." "God is far removed." You know the type of imagery I'm talking about. It is a picture of God that makes him void of compassion and full of wrath and anger. It is for this reason that many people do not even bother crossing the threshold of his house anymore with the exceptions of funerals, weddings, Christmas, or Easter.

But wait! If that's you and you have given up on or chosen to ignore God the Father, then please hear me out. I promise you two things. The first is this: I won't bore you with a whole bunch of theological jargon and esoteric "churchese" for which you need a special dictionary. Yes, I will talk about God. I will talk about Jesus. I may occasionally bring in the mysterious third member of the dynamic trio, the Holy Spirit. But what I want is to simply illuminate Jesus' beautiful picture of his Father through stories, humor and relevant everyday talk.

Secondly, I promise that I will do my best to present an easily understandable picture of Jesus' explanation as to the nature of God the Father. My aim is to capture this picture that Jesus is painting so clearly you'd have to be wearing headphones to miss out on it. No, wait a second. Headphones would stop you from hearing, not reading. What I am trying to say is that I don't want you to be scratching your head wondering, "Now is that a bush or porcupine? No wait! It's Bob Ross's overgrown hair!" So you can count on me to work as hard as I can to make this picture clear as day.

But while I commit myself to this hard work, I'd like to ask you in turn to make me a deal. It may be one of the harder things you've done, but I promise it will also be one of the most rewarding. I'd like you to take a blank canvas in your mind and say to God, "Okay, I'm going to let you paint a picture of who you *really* are through the words of Jesus." Then give Jesus a fair chance to convince you that the Father in heaven you have heard about is truly the most amazing being in the entire universe. If you have the courage to start afresh and pull out that new canvas, I have faith you will be pleasantly surprised by the masterpiece at the end.

WHY JESUS?

Perhaps you may be considering my proposition and asking yourself, "Why Jesus? Why should I listen to the testimony of Jesus about who God is, anyway? I mean, after all, isn't Jesus as the painter somewhat biased about the topic? Won't he just tell us all the good things and keep away the bad? Will we get the real low down on who God is or just a bunch more religious dogma that drove me away from church or at least kept me from adding the title of Father or the adjective good to the name God?"

Let me explain why I believe Jesus is the most credible source to paint the picture of God. First of all, Jesus is honest. For some people that may go without saying, but others need a bit more explanation, so let me give it. As we study the life of Jesus for even a short time, we begin to understand that he is

JESUS WAS NEVER A PEOPLE PLEASER. HE WAS AND IS HONEST AND FORTHRIGHT.

quite frank. Maybe frank is too casual a word to call Jesus. Let's try forthright. Yes, Jesus is probably the most forthright person I have ever encountered. In fact at times I'd say he is embarrassingly and painfully straightforward. Jesus speaks his mind in such a way that can make us either pink with blush or red in the face with anger. We are either melted by his compassionate deeds and stories or on edge by his righteous claims. In either case, Jesus was never a people pleaser. He was and is honest and forthright. He is going to tell you what's on his mind. He'll be straight up with you.

The second reason to immerse ourselves in the words of Jesus is that he seems to know what he's talking about when it comes to the topic of God. If I am seeking advice, I want it to come from the right person. If I am at the library, I ask the librarian where to find a book. If I am getting my car fixed, I ask my mechanic what is going on under the hood.

Now if I asked my librarian how to fix my car, she might send me down the aisle to a book entitled *How to Fix Cars for Dummies*. But believe me, no book on car repair can help this dummy! I'm happy if I can figure out how to fill my tank with the right type of gas. Conversely, if I asked my mechanic where to find a certain book, if he's smart, he'll tell me to ask the librarian.

My point is simple. When we need advice, we ought to ask the expert. In the case of God, Jesus claims to be the most qualified expert on the block. Just listen to Jesus' words on the topic of God the Father:

> All things have been handed over to me by my Father, and no one knows the Son except the Father, and no one knows the Father except the Son and anyone to whom the Son chooses to reveal him.[1]

Like I said previously, Jesus is not one to give you some pat expression and send you on your way. He speaks boldly about himself and about his relationship with God. Just take his above statement, for example. What an audacious and amazing statement for Jesus to make about himself and his relationship with God! First of all, he says that all things have been handed over to him by God. That includes God's authority, his people, his judgments, everything.[2] In essence, Jesus is saying, "God has put me in charge." That's quite a statement to make about yourself, don't you think? But wait, he goes further.

---

1   Matthew 11:27
2   See Matthew 28:18, John 10:25-30, John 6:37-40, John 5:22, 27, John 3:35 and John 13:3.

Jesus goes on to say that nobody knows him except the Father, and nobody knows the Father except the Son. Jesus is saying that the relationship he has with God the Father is not like any other relationship. It is closer than the most intimate relationship between a man and a woman. It is more exclusive than the words of a binding contract between two parties. Jesus and the Father are deeply connected to one another with no middleman (or middle-woman) in between—with one important exception. Jesus says, "no one knows the Father except the Son **and** anyone to whom the Son chooses **to reveal** him."

In other words, Jesus has added one clause to this exclusive contract between the Father and Son. Jesus has exclusive rights to knowing God the Father, but he is also willing to reveal the Father to those he chooses. Now we're getting somewhere. In fact, the premise of this book is straightforward. Jesus knows the Father best, so if we want to meet the Father, we need to ask Jesus for an introduction.

JESUS KNOWS THE FATHER BEST, SO IF WE WANT TO MEET THE FATHER, WE NEED TO ASK JESUS FOR AN INTRODUCTION.

What makes this even more interesting is that the word "reveal" here in our English Bibles is actually translated from a Greek word meaning "to take off the cover or disclose".[3] It can also mean, "to make known" or "discover what before was unknown".[4] So what Jesus is telling us is that he has the ability and authority to take the cover off the mystery of God the Father, so we can truly know him for ourselves.

Picture in your mind's eye a magician who has a red cloth covering an object on a stand. In one quick swoop of the cloth, it comes off to reveal something amazing underneath, a live bunny or a pigeon or some other fluffy or feathered creature. Jesus is promising that he has the ability to take the cover off so we can see God for ourselves.

Or picture instead the cover Jesus is about to take off is the cover of a pool. Summer is about to begin, and the cover needs to come off so we can enjoy a refreshing dip. Similarly, Jesus wants to remove

3   Strong's Greek Dictionary #601.
4   Blue Letter Bible website, accessed January 23, 2017,
      https://www.blueletterbible.org/lang/lexicon/lexicon.cfm?t=kjv&strongs=g601

the cover from our eyes so that we not only see the beauty of God the Father, but may also jump into his everlasting arms and enjoy a dip in the spiritual pool of life.

Let's add one more image. This one is of our good friend Bob Ross standing before one of his beautiful paintings. The painting cannot be seen because there is a black cloth draped over the top of the easel. The crowd is gathered around to see his most recent painting. On a count of 3, 2, 1 the cloth is whisked away, and the crowd simultaneously exclaims in awe, "OOOOOHH"!

Jesus' mission is to take off the cover and mystery behind knowing God the Father so that we can all stand in awe and wonder at the goodness of God for ourselves. Get ready for something amazing.

HOW, JESUS?

Once we understand why Jesus is the source of the answers we seek about the Father, we then have to ask the question how. How will Jesus paint this beautiful and irresistible picture of God the Father? Jesus revealed the Father in two primary ways. The first was through the miracles Jesus performed. Jesus said:

> But if I do his work, believe in the evidence of the miraculous works I have done, even if you don't believe me. Then you will know and understand that the Father is in me, and I am in the Father.[5]

The miraculous works that Jesus performed while here on earth were evidence for observers to see that Jesus was indeed one with God the Father. In fact, Jesus went so far as to encourage people **not** to believe in him unless he performed the works of the Father: "Do not believe me unless I do the works of my Father."[6]

MIRACLE AFTER MIRACLE, KIND DEED AFTER KIND DEED, MERCY UPON MERCY, JESUS WAS SHOWING US THAT THE FATHER TRULY IS GOOD.

Jesus' statements testify to his own deity and personhood. He is in essence saying, "Look at the miracles I do and realize that I and God are one and the same." That

5   John 10:28, New Living Translation
6   John 10:37, New Living Translation, see also John 14:11

is quite an audacious and powerful statement. The miracles Jesus performed were also indicators of what the Father is like. Don't miss this point! Every time Jesus healed blind eyes, made lame men walk, embraced social outcasts and sinners with love, and even when he turned water into wine, he was saying to the world: "This is what my Father is like!" Miracle after miracle, kind deed after kind deed, mercy upon mercy, Jesus was showing us that the Father truly is good.

The second way in which Jesus reveals the Father to us is through his words. Jesus talked incessantly about the nature of his Father and his Father's goodness towards all humanity. This second way that Jesus revealed the Father will be the primary focus of this book. We will explore Jesus' words to better understand the picture he is painting, so that we can step back, pause, and reflect on what we are seeing, or simply stand in awe. So get out your blank canvas and get ready. Jesus is about to paint something fascinating and beautiful.

Points to Remember:

- Jesus is honest.
- Jesus knows the Father best.
- Jesus came to reveal the Father to us.

Prayer:

"God, I choose to give you a blank canvas. I am open to allowing Jesus to paint a new picture of you."

Meditation:

Jesus reveals the Father.

Group Discussion:

- How would you describe your childhood understanding of God?
- Which view of God are you most likely to embrace today: Authoritarian, Benevolent, Critical, Distant or Non-Existent?
- Complete this sentence: If God were like my paternal Father, I would describe him as _____.

Dig Deeper:

Read through the following verses to learn more about Jesus' relationship with the Father.

- John 7:29: I know him because I am from him and he sent me.
- John 8:42: Jesus said to them, "If God were your Father, you would love me, for I have come here from God. I have not come on my own; God sent me."
- John 8:55: Though you do not know him, I know him. If I said I did not, I would be a liar like you, but I do know him and obey his word.
- John 13:3: Jesus knew that the Father had put all things under his power, and that he had come from God and was returning to God.
- John 16:28: I came from the Father and entered the world; now I am leaving the world and going back to the Father.

CHAPTER TWO

A FATHER WHO PROVIDES

"If you have a special need today, focus your full attention on the goodness and greatness of your Father rather than on the size of your need. Your need is tiny compared to His ability to meet it."

— BILL PATTERSON

One of the greatest privileges I have as a father is to provide for my kids' needs. Just yesterday I took my oldest son Elijah to Wal-Mart. We went to purchase one item—paper for our home computer. The paper is located in one of the back aisles, so to get there we had to pass three zillion yellow smiley face stickers marking discounted products. I don't think I've ever successfully left Wal-Mart without purchasing at least several additional items and spending double the amount of money I had originally planned to spend.

So after grabbing a couple of packs of printer paper, my son and I began to weave our way towards the front register. It was like making our way through a discount landmine. Elijah and I were trudging through this low-price labyrinth when his eyes fell upon some Philadelphia Eagles slippers. Now the Eagles are the hometown favorite professional American football team where we reside in Pennsylvania, but they hadn't exactly been shining on the field in recent years. The biggest surprise to me was that after a terrible season for the Birds, these slippers were not discounted. Sometimes life just doesn't make any sense. I balked at the bird slippers because they looked terribly uncomfortable, kind of like watching the Eagle's football season this year—ouch!

We were able to find a different pair of slippers that were a better fit and more comfortable. At which point my son informed me that many of his socks had holes in them. It certainly doesn't help that my kids enjoy running around outside in their socks, something I just do not understand. I digress.

In any case, when Elijah told me his socks had holes in them, my dad pride puffed up nice and strong, and I said something to the effect, "No son of mine is going to go around with holes in his socks!" An age-old expression like "no son of mine" made me feel like a real father—old school style. Elijah and I walked back down the maze to find the sock aisle. After a little searching, we found my son some new socks.

As we were leaving, my son turned to me and said in earnest the three words every father wants to hear from their son or daughter: "Thank you, Dad!" That is really all I needed to hear. In fact, if my kids want to make me happy, that's all they'd need to say to me. They could even shorten it to "Thanks, Dad!", and I would be content. Heck, they could say it in Spanish—"Gracias, Papá"—or Portuguese—"Obrigado, Papai!"—or German—"Danke, Vater!"—and I would be perfectly happy, and I don't even speak those languages.

DON'T WORRY, BE HAPPY

Our Father in Heaven loves to provide for our needs, and he simply wants to hear us say, "Thank you, Daddy." That's it. It's nothing too radical, just a simple thank you. Practice it even now and feel the joy there is in giving thanks to the Father. Breathe in nice and deep, and then slowly say these words, "Thank you, Father." Practice that habit regularly and you will surely find greater peace in your heart.

Jesus knew his Father to be a provider, and he had a lot to say about his Father's ability to provide:

Therefore, I tell you, do not worry about your life, what you will eat or drink; or about your body, what you will wear. Is not life more than food, and the body more than clothes? Look at the birds of the air; they do not sow or reap or store away in barns, and yet your heavenly Father feeds them. Are you not much more valuable than they? Can any one of you by worrying add a single hour to your life? And why do you worry about clothes?

See how the flowers of the field grow. They do not labor or spin. Yet I tell you that not even Solomon in all his splendor was dressed like one of these. If that is how God clothes the grass of the field, which is here today and tomorrow is thrown into the fire, will he not much more clothe you—you of little faith?[1]

Let me ask you some introspective questions:

- What's had you most worried in recent days?
- What has kept you up at night?
- What has occupied more of your mind and heart than is deserved?

Jesus gives us some straightforward and basic advice: "Do not worry about your life." Pretty simple, right? Well, simple, yet so challenging for most of us! How do we actually live a life of no worry, a life that is carefree and full of gladness? Jesus has an answer to our question. He points to nature as our guide.

Jesus tells us to observe the birds of the sky. "You see them?" Jesus exhorts us, "My Father feeds them every single day." Now let me ask you, when was the last time you saw a bird that looked worried? In fact, birds are often symbols of freedom, peace and levity ... unless of course we're talking about the Philadelphia Eagles!

Jesus tells us that it's God the Father who feeds the birds. Remember that blank canvas we spoke about at the start of our journey? Picture on that canvas an open hand full of bird seed. Now join me in imagining little birds approaching one by one to feed out of that hand. What a beautiful picture of grace and love being displayed towards these small creatures of nature! But the amazing thing about this picture is that it's not a human hand feeding these birds. It is our all-powerful Father God who created the heavens and earth. As the Psalms so poignantly say, "You open your hand and satisfy the desires of every living thing."[2] And again the Psalms declare, "He gives food to every living thing. His faithful love endures forever."[3]

Just consider that God the Father with all his great creative power and might is merciful and kind enough to feed these tiny birds. Jesus

---

1   Matthew 6:25-30

2   Psalm 145:16

3   Psalm 136:25, New Living Translation

follows up on the above illustration with one of his famous rhetorical questions: *"Are you not much more valuable than they?"* Here is a great question to ponder. Are you of more value to God than a bird? I sure hope your answer is an unequivocal yes, but in case it's not, let me unravel some of the depths of this one question.

IN HIS IMAGE AND LIKENESS

In the beginning, the Father along with the Son and the Spirit created all things for their glory—the birds, the sun, the sky, the earth, and even happy little trees. After each thing that God created in the universe, he looked upon his own marvelous work and proclaimed, "It is good!" The canvas of all creation was pleasing in God's sight, and he congratulated himself on a job well done. While God was admiring all of creation, the mammals, the fish, the birds, and even the reptiles, he said to himself:

> Let us make mankind in our image, in our likeness, so that they may rule over the fish in the sea and the birds in the sky, over the livestock and all the wild animals, and over all the creatures that move along the ground.[4]

God created a picture perfect world full of colors and sounds and living creatures. It was an original, better by far than a Bob Ross painting. When God looked upon this beautiful world, my guess is that he thought to himself: "There is something missing and I know just what it is. I need to create someone like me who can enjoy this beautiful creation of mine."

In enters man. God in his imagination created mankind in his own image and likeness. Of all the beautiful things God had created, this one creation would be separate, different, and distinct because God created it with a picture of himself in mind. It was no longer an abstract world of living objects. This creation would now be much closer to a self-portrait: "This creation of mine is going to resemble me!"

GOD DID NOT JUST CREATE US FOR HIMSELF. HE CREATED US LIKE HIMSELF!

So God looked at himself in a mirror as he created mankind. "Let's see, I want to give them my ability to think, imagine, dream, create,

4   Genesis 1:26

choose, develop, and rule over all of my creation." <u>God did not just create us *for* himself. He created us *like* himself!</u> It is no surprise why King David, when he wrote Psalm 139, said, "I praise you because I am fearfully and wonderfully made; your works are wonderful, I know that full well."[5]

Now let's traverse back to Jesus' rhetorical question. "Are you not much more valuable than they?" In this one short question, Jesus is making a statement, a declaration, even a constitution. Allow me to paraphrase for a moment: "Hey guys, don't you get it? Don't you know you were created in the very image of God? I mean, my Father took the time to create you like us, and when God made you he had us in mind. You are important to him, so much more important than the little birds of the sky. Don't you know this already? Don't you understand just how important your life is to my Father?"

Hopefully, most of us can nod our heads and say, "Yeah, sure. I get that. I am more important than a bird in the sky. Okay, I can accept that, Jesus."

Conceptually, it's not difficult to understand how our lives are more valuable than the life of a bird, a plant, or a fish. Yet we can easily lose this connection when our bills are piled high, the stock market plunges, a pink slip removes our sense of financial security, or we estimate the future costs of our children's college education or our retirement. In those moments, we have the choice to believe we are greater than the birds or we can dismiss the words of Jesus and consider God's promises as being "for the birds".

The question is worth asking: "Does God really care about my problems, both big and small?" Jesus makes a bird-to-man connection in another portion of Scripture when he states:

> "Are not two sparrows sold for a penny? Yet not one of them will fall to the ground outside your Father's care. And even the very hairs of your head are all numbered."[6]

Birds were the one pet I had as a child. I was content with them. I didn't need a dog or a cat. I was fascinated with birds and their majestic ability to fly. We never had any of the expensive talking birds,

5   Psalm 139:14, NIV
6   Matthew 10:29-30

just ordinary parakeets which seem to be the cheapest type of bird money can buy. In Jesus' day, a sparrow was the cheapest bird in town. For a couple of Roman pennies, you could have your own pair, though in that era Jews actually used them for food, not as pets, and they were seen as being of little value.

In speaking of sparrows, Jesus gives us insight to the Father's knowledge of all things (omniscience) and care for all creation: "Yet not one (sparrow) will fall to the ground outside your Father's care." God has his eye upon the most insignificant of all creation. He also has his eyes on the very hairs of our head. In fact, he has them all numbered. Comparatively speaking, the hairs of our head and the birds of the air are in direct correlation to the worries of our life.

IF GOD CARES ABOUT THE THINGS WE FIND TO BE TRIVIAL AND INSIGNIFICANT, BY CONTRAST HE HAS EVEN GREATER CARE FOR THE THINGS THAT WEIGH US DOWN.

Jesus is telling us in these verses that God cares about things we don't even bother to worry about or notice, like the bird that dies in the forest and the hair we unknowingly (or knowingly!) lost today. If God cares about things we find to be trivial and insignificant, by contrast he has even greater care for those things that weigh us down, making our hairs turn gray and making us feel like flying the coop.

FOOD AND CLOTHING

I would imagine that Jesus' audience had both men and women. "Is not life more than food and the body more than clothing?" must have been directed to both genders. Men think a lot about food. If you ever want to entice men to come to a church event, just use one of these three "b" words in your promotion: breakfast, barbeque or burgers. That tends to draw a male crowd pretty fast. And if you ever throw in the fourth "b" word, bacon, you better break out more chairs because men love anything with bacon on it. I'm sure I could convince a man to watch the ballet if there was a promise of bacon during intermission. "Bacon? I'm there!"

In contrast, in my observation at least, the average woman tends to think a lot more about clothing than most of the men I know. Have you ever seen a man sitting in a chair waiting for his wife to try on a

13

new dress? Let me cue you in. That man feels like he's being tortured! Empathize with the brother. Let him cry on your shoulder or at least hand him a piece of bacon to ease his pain.

It never ceases to amaze me how a woman can enter a walk-in closet full of clothing and say, "I have nothing to wear!" and a man can open up a refrigerator full of food and say, "There is nothing to eat!" *Vive la différence!*

In speaking to us about these basic necessities, Jesus says, "Do not worry". In other words, he is telling us: "Men, do not worry about what you will have for dinner. I know you are hungry, but you will not starve. Ladies, do not worry about what you will wear to work, church, dinner or even to the mall to go shopping for more clothes. You will find something to wear, even if it's not your favorite outfit in the world. You won't go without clothes."

Abraham Maslow was an American psychologist who developed a theory now known as "Maslow's hierarchy of needs". In this hierarchy, often pictured as a pyramid, a person's most basic needs are at the base. These needs include essentials like breathing, food, clothing, and sleep. Next in his paradigm is the need for safety—whether physical, financial, family or property. Third in the chain of needs and closer to the top of the pyramid is love and belonging. We can all relate to the needs of acceptance among family and friends. Following our needs for love and belonging is the need for esteem, both for ourselves and the respect of others. Finally, at the top of the pyramid is "self-actualization", which includes virtues such as creativity, morality, spontaneity, problem solving, lack of prejudice, and acceptance of facts.

I appreciate Maslow's work, not because I wholeheartedly believe that the paradigm he constructed is inherently true for all people, but because it provides a simple model by which we can better understand and evaluate human needs. If I were to meet a poor, homeless man on the streets of New York, it would make sense that he is more interested in having his next meal than whether or not he will find self-actualization or his life's purpose. He is first focused on his lowest level of need before he can reach for anything much higher.

In this context, Jesus' words bring a new sense of depth to our present view of reality. "Is not *life* more than food, and the body more than clothes?" The word life used in the Greek text is *psuche*, meaning "breath, (by implication) spirit, abstractly or concretely".[7] In other portions of the New Testament, when this word is used, it is translated as "soul". Here are a few examples from Jesus' own words:

> *And fear not them who kill the body, but are not able to kill the soul:*[8]

> *Take my yoke upon you, and learn of me; for I am meek and lowly in heart: and you shall find rest unto your souls.*[9]

> *For what is a man profited, if he shall gain the whole world, and lose his own soul? or what shall a man give in exchange for his soul?*[10]

Jesus is asking his listeners whether or not we understand that our lives are deeper than the basic needs of food and clothing. Do we understand that our bodies are just a physical representation of the soul we carry? We are not like the happy little trees, the mountains, or the grass of the field. We are not even like the most sophisticated and intelligent animals. We have souls that have been created by God and will live together with him for eternity. We are made in his image. For this reason, life is more than the amount of calories we consume in a day and whether or not we are wearing the latest in fashion.

To put it in Maslow's terminology, we have a greater hierarchy of existence or needs than just that which sustains and covers our flesh. We are meant for higher purposes in this life and the next. We are destined for relationship with God the Father. We are called to be his sons and daughters, not just his creation. We are called to a place of spiritual depth and vitality that cannot be known by other living creatures.

CAN WORRY ADD TO LIFE?

At the end of the day, we have to ask ourselves the question: "What is worry doing for me?" Is it helping me pay my bills? Is it making me a more productive person? Is it making any of my circumstances better?

---

7   Strong's Greek Dictionary, #5590.
8   Matthew 10:28a
9   Matthew 11:29
10 Matthew 16:26

Does worry add any value to my existence? As Jesus put it: *"Can any one of you by worrying add a single hour to your life?"*

A study was conducted of 1600 men ages 43 to 91 to examine the relationship between a neurotic personality and life expectancy. The study found that men who had an increased neuroticism over time were more likely to die sooner: "Even a small increase in neuroticism over the course of the study led to a 40% increase in death compared to a stable person."[11]

RESEARCH BACKS UP WHAT JESUS TAUGHT OVER 2000 YEARS AGO – WORRY TAKES AWAY YEARS OF LIFE INSTEAD OF ADDING TO IT.

So in terms of longevity, research backs up what Jesus taught over 2000 years ago -i.e. that worry takes away years of life instead of adding to it. Worry does not stop there. Worry and stress have an effect on our bodies, mood, and behavior. The Mayo Clinic states: "Stress left unchecked can contribute to health problems such as high blood pressure, heart disease, obesity, and diabetes."[12] Stress and worry can also affect our emotions, causing lack of motivation and focus, irritability, anger, sadness, and even depression. It can lead to behavioral habits such as overeating, drug and alcohol abuse, or social withdrawal.[13]

It should now be clear that worry adds all the wrong things to our lives. So, why do we bother worrying? Some may say it is habitual. Others may say it's in their blood. Still others may point to the amount of pressure in their life to perform, produce, and get results. All the while, the birds of the air are living carefree!

SEEK GOD'S KINGDOM

So what can we do to change our neurotic behaviors and tendencies, turning them into trophies of God's amazing grace? Here is Jesus' conclusion and answer:

11 Worry and Anxiety Impact Longevity, About.com,
    http://longevity.about.com/od/longevityandillness/a/neurotic_worry.htm,
    accessed April 8, 2015
12 Mayo Clinic, Stress Symptoms: Effects on your body and behavior,
    http://www.mayoclinic.org/healthyliving/stress-management/in-depth/stress-symptoms/art-20050987?pg=1, Accessed April 8, 2015
13 Ibid. Accessed, April 8, 2015.

So do not worry, saying, "What shall we eat?" or "What shall we drink?" or "What shall we wear?" For the pagans run after all these things, and your heavenly Father knows that you need them. But seek first his kingdom and his righteousness, and all these things will be given to you as well. Therefore do not worry about tomorrow, for tomorrow will worry about itself. Each day has enough trouble of its own.[14]

If his Jewish audience was not shocked enough by Jesus comparing their lives to meager sparrows, then they surely felt the weight of these words. In essence, Jesus is saying: "You are running around like people with no faith, wondering if your Father is going to take care of you. You sound like a bunch of pagans! Don't you know that Our Good Father is fully aware of the things you need?" Jesus again used the p-word when he taught his disciples how to pray:

*And when you pray, do not keep on babbling like **pagans**, for they think they will be heard because of their many words. Do not be like them, for your Father knows what you need before you ask him.[15]*

Our Good Father knows the things we need even before we ask him for them. When Abraham was tested by God to see if he would obediently offer his only son Isaac on the altar, Abraham put full confidence in God's ability to provide a sacrifice in place of his son.[16] After the Lord provided a ram in the thicket, Abraham gave a name to the place where he had offered up his son in recognition of God's divine act of provision. He called the place "Jehovah-jireh".

Many of our English Bibles translate "Jehovah-jireh" to read "The Lord will provide". If we have studied this passage in church or a Bible study, we may have been taught to equate the name Jehovah-Jireh with "God our Provider". Yet if we look into the meaning of the original Hebrew, the words actually translate: "Jehovah will see (to it)".[17] In other words, God already sees what you have need of before you ever ask him to provide! Again referring to pagans, Jesus taught

---

14 Matthew 6:31-34

15 Matthew 6:7-8

16 Genesis 22:1-19

17 Strong's Hebrew Dictionary, #3070

us, "Do not be like them, for your Father knows what you need before you ask him."[18]

Not only does Father God see what we need, **he cares for what we need**. A God who sees a need, but has no empathy or compassion for that need, is worse than a God who cannot see the need at all. The Bible teaches us that the Father who created us not only sees our needs, but his heart feels the emotional weight of those needs and his compassion draws his attention to our needs.

GOD ALREADY SEES WHAT YOU HAVE NEED OF BEFORE YOU EVER ASK HIM TO PROVIDE!

If the belief in God the Father being a provider were only a theology on paper, it would not be sufficient. Fortunately, my real-life experience, along with countless other children of God, matches the testimony of Jesus' words. God truly does provide for our needs. I have been the recipient of so many blessings that were undoubtedly sent from heaven by my Father.

One story in particular comes to mind that has never ceased to amaze me. My wife and I were married for less than two years; we had our first child, Elijah, and were trying to establish our family. I was working in Corporate America, but finances were still quite tight in those early years. Through a series of events, I felt like God wanted me to go on a mission trip to Ghana, Africa. The problem was that I needed money for the trip, beginning with a $500 deposit.

We agreed that if God truly was orchestrating this trip, he would need to provide for my expenses, starting with the deposit. I prayed, fasted, asked, hoped and believed God to provide for my needs. On the last day possible to submit the deposit, I received a check in the mail from my insurance company. To this day, I still have no idea why they sent me the check; I had not submitted a claim or had any other reason that they owed me money. The check was written for $500 even, the exact amount I needed for the deposit. In the weeks leading up to the trip, God was faithful to provide every last penny needed to go on the trip through many generous people. God not only provided the funds, he made the trip to Africa a life-changing experience for me!

---

18 Matthew 6:8

While unbelievers are running around worrying about their life's needs, Jesus tells his followers to instead "seek first his kingdom and righteousness, and all these things will be given to you as well." Our Father not only sees what we need and cares about it, but he provides in abundance for what we need.

Our responsibility is to simply come to him in pure faith as a child comes to their earthly father, asking him not only for what we need, but that we may see his kingdom and his will be done on this earth. If we become concerned with God's agenda, he promises to take care of our needs and even many of our wants and desires. If God cares for the birds and the grass, won't he care for you? Or as I said to my son Elijah, so the Father says to you: "No child of mine is going to go around with holes in his socks!"

Points to Remember:

- Father God **knows** what you need.
- Father God **cares** for what you need.
- Father God **provides** for what you need.

Prayer:

"Father God, thank you for the ways you have provided for me and will continue to meet my every need."

Meditation:

Our Good Father provides for his kids.

Group Discussion:

- What do you tend to worry about the most?
- What would life be like if you lived completely free of any worry or anxiety?
- How have you seen God provide for you in times past?

Dig Deeper:

Read through the following verses to study more about God's provision for his children.

- Matthew 6:26: Look at the birds of the air; they do not sow or reap or store away in barns, and yet your heavenly Father feeds them. Are you not much more valuable than they?
- Philippians 4:19 KJV: But my God shall supply all your need according to his riches in glory by Christ Jesus.
- Matthew 10:29-30: Are not two sparrows sold for a penny? Yet not one of them will fall to the ground outside your Father's care. And even the very hairs of your head are all numbered.
- Matthew 6:31-34: So do not worry, saying, "What shall we eat?" or "What shall we drink?" or "What shall we wear?" For the pagans run after all these things, and your heavenly Father knows that you need them. But seek first his kingdom and his righteousness, and all these things will be given to you as well. Therefore do not worry about tomorrow, for tomorrow will worry about itself. Each day has enough trouble of its own.

CHAPTER THREE

A FATHER WHO REWARDS

"God is a good paymaster; He pays His servants while at work as well as when they have done it."

— CHARLES HADDON SPURGEON

One of the most memorable experiences I had as a kid was working for my dad. My father was the second-generation owner of Eade's Distributing Company Inc., a beverage distributorship in our small hometown, Olean, New York. In the summers, as a young boy, I had the honor of working in my dad's warehouse. My main job was to stack cases of beer, juice, and "pop" (the upstate New York word for soda) onto wooden pallets that would later be delivered to supermarkets, convenience stores, and bars.

Admittedly, I was at times more of a liability than an asset for my father's business. One day in my later teens, I was maneuvering a forklift to pick up a full pallet of beer. Making a judgment error, I came in too high with the forklift's metal prongs, or "forks". When I did, I punctured several cases of beer at the bottom of the pallet. Beer began to ooze out of the punctured cases. I ended up having to break down the entire pallet one case at a time in order to remove the broken cases at the bottom. After cleaning up the beer mess, I then had to put the undamaged cases back on the pallet. All this was being done on the clock, so I was in essence being paid to remedy my own mistakes.

My favorite day of the work week was payday, which for us was every Friday. I loved getting paid. Some things hold true at any age! At the end of my Friday shift, I would climb up the staircase that led to my father's office area. His secretary, Robin, would calculate the number of hours I had worked that week on an oversized desk calculator that spat out paper with the calculations. She would multiply my hours by five (my wage per hour), then place stone cold cash into my eager adolescent hands. Oh how I loved Fridays!

In hindsight, I find something incredibly generous about my father's willingness to employ me. Here I was, a young boy with a less than average work ethic and minimal skill set, being paid by my father who already supplied everything I owned and enjoyed in life. Every ounce of food I ate, every piece of clothing on my back, and every basketball camp I ever attended was fully funded by my dad. Yet he was willing to employ me for wages instead of just making me labor as compensation for his provision of my room, board and basketball.

ENTITLEMENT, PERFORMANCE AND REWARD

In our current era of entitlement and worker's rights, it might sound only fair and just for my dad to pay me to work. But there was a day when sons were required to work in their father's fields or workshop, laboring all day just to help feed the family, not to pad their own personal bank account. In contrast my dad's willingness to pay me, on top of the fact that he was already providing everything I owned and enjoyed, was an amazing act of graciousness and love. It is like parents who give their kids an allowance. If life were all about fairness and not about love, then just "allowing" your kids to eat, sleep, and lounge in your home would be more than a fair allowance.

Our understanding of God's nature affects how we approach him in prayer. If we have an attitude of entitlement, we approach God with an "I deserve it!" mentality. We want what we want when we want it, and by the way, we want it now! Maintaining such arrogance is difficult if we possess even the slightest degree of reverence towards the Almighty. It is like putting your feet up on the kitchen table and telling your mom, "Feed me dinner!"

On the other side of the spectrum, we can find ourselves striving to perform in an attempt to pay God back for what he's already done in our life, to earn his favor, or just in the hope that he will like us. We too often see ourselves as indebted slaves instead of beloved children of Our Good Father.

The truth is that we can never repay God for what he has done for us in Christ. The debt of sin that Jesus died for is greater than anything we could ever pay back to God in return. Surprisingly, God in his graciousness and generosity actually wants to pay us in return for our labors. The Father wants to give us more and better than we deserve. Jesus taught it this way:

> Be careful not to practice your righteousness in front of others to be seen by them. If you do, you will have no **reward** from your Father in heaven. So when you give to the needy, do not announce it with trumpets, as the hypocrites do in the synagogues and on the streets, to be honored by others. Truly I tell you, they have received their **reward** in full. But when you give to the needy, do not let your left hand know what your right hand is doing, so that your giving may be in secret. Then your Father, who sees what is done in secret, will **reward** you.[1]

The word translated "reward" in this passage comes from a Greek word meaning, "pay for service, hire, reward, wages."[2] The word reward is not describing a free gift, but something that is earned by one's work. We could actually use the words "pay, payment, or paycheck" in replacement of these words to help us make better sense of Jesus' teaching. "Your Father, who sees what is done in secret, will *pay you*."

> GOD IS TOO GENEROUS AND TOO KIND TO NOT REWARD US FOR THE LABOR WE WORK IN HIS NAME.

We might consider the idea of being paid by God as downright heretical nonsense. How on earth does God owe us anything? He does not need to pay us for a thing! He has already given us his very best by allowing his son Jesus to die on the cross for our sins. We did not deserve that gift, and by no means do we deserve to be paid by God!

---

1   Matthew 6:1-4, emphasis mine.
2   Strong's Concordance, #3408

23

I personally could not agree more with this line of thinking. We are indebted to the graciousness of God more than we will ever really know, understand, or comprehend. So why on earth should the gracious God who gave his only Son Jesus to die for us on the cross pay us in return for our good deeds?

The truth is that there is no reason he should. It doesn't make sense. It is unjust in the economy of what seems fair. But that is exactly what makes it so amazing.

While it is only right and just for us to give everything in our lives back to God and expect nothing in return, God is too generous and too kind *not* to reward his children for whatever labor we undertake in his name. This is just another sign of God's amazing grace. When we go out and do good of any kind in the world, God smiles down from heaven and thinks to himself, "I really want to reward my child for a job well done!"

And who are we to argue with God? If God desires to shower us with his goodness, grace and love, then who am I to say he cannot? It reminds me of a story from the life of the apostle Peter. Peter was an ambitious character, one who had a great amount of zeal and passion. Personally, I can relate a lot to this guy.

At the end of Jesus' life, he calls together his twelve closest followers for a final meal. Things seem to be going according to plan when Jesus pulls out a bucket of water. He bends down to his friends' dirty, smelly feet and begins to wash them. Now, washing someone's feet was an act of servitude and humility more typically reserved for servants and those of lower status (or the woman of the house if no one else was available!).

The reason for foot-washing was obvious enough in an era before paved streets and wheeled transportation. Guests arrived at a house with sandals and dirt-caked feet from the dusty roads and were expected to wash off before stepping into someone's clean home or lounging on spotless cushions and mats. That Jesus was the one to step forward would indicate not only that there were no servants or host available, but that none of his disciples had volunteered for such a lowly task. In any case, washing people's feet was hardly a task to which the Lord of heaven should have to stoop. Peter was well aware of this and had the audacity to tell Jesus just how he felt about it:

He came to Simon Peter, who said to him, "Lord, are you going to wash my feet?" Jesus replied, "You do not realize now what I am doing, but later you will understand." "No," said Peter, "you shall never wash my feet."[3]

Can you hear Peter's determination here? "You shall **never** wash my feet." Peter was refusing to allow Jesus to serve him. Why? Peter understood that he was unworthy to be served in such humility by the one who he considered his Savior and Master. In essence, he was saying, "No way, no how, you are not going to humble yourself in this way when you have already done so much for me! I should be washing *your* feet!"

Jesus gave Peter a pretty stern ultimatum, "Unless I wash you, you have no part with me."[4] Peter could choose to opt out of the foot washing. Or he could allow Jesus to wash his feet as Jesus had done for the other disciples. Peter quickly changed his mind, pleading instead for the Lord to wash his entire body.[5]

Get this! God the Father wants to bless you. He wants to bring good things into your life. He wants to reward you and pay you back for everything you do in his name. He wants to give you more than what you deserve because if you got what you deserved, you'd be on the highway to hell. God actually wants to pay you for your service to him, not because he has to or because you earned it on your own, but because he is gracious, kind, generous and more than just fair.

"Therefore, my dear brothers and sisters, stand firm. Let nothing move you. Always give yourselves fully to the work of the Lord, because you know that your labor in the Lord is not in vain."[6]

"Whatever you do, do your work heartily, as for the Lord rather than for men, knowing that from the Lord you will receive the reward of the inheritance. It is the Lord Christ whom you serve."[7]

WHO GETS THE CREDIT?

There is only one major stipulation here. When you help the old lady cross the street, when you take the time to volunteer at church, when

3   John 13:6-8a
4   John 13:8b
5   John 13:1-9
6   1 Corinthians 15:58
7   Colossians 3:23-24

you serve the poor at a local food kitchen, God wants you to do these deeds not so that people will admire you, but so that they will admire him. God wants the publicity not to focus on you and your good efforts, but on him and his incredible benevolence.

As we saw in the above passage, the religious leaders of Jesus' day did everything for show. They dressed for show. They fed the poor for show. They prayed for show. It was all one big show. In fact, the word "hypocrite" that Jesus used to describe these men actually means "an actor under an assumed character".[8] Like professional actors, these men were in it for two reasons—to be seen by others and to be honored by others.

Jesus teaches that when we seek honor from mankind, then we get honor from mankind alone. But if we seek to honor God the Father, then God opens up the windows of heaven and pours out his blessing upon us, both now and in eternity. It all comes down to motives. Jesus is teaching us that the Father is someone who looks deeper than meets the eye. The Father is looking upon the heart:

> But the Lord said to Samuel, "Do not consider his appearance or his height, for I have rejected him. The Lord does not look at the things people look at. People look at the outward appearance, but **the Lord looks at the heart**."[9]

HOW ABOUT THEM APPLES?

I like red apples, the redder the better. When I see a shiny red apple, especially one that has been slightly chilled, my mouth begins to water. Boy, do I like red apples! The local convenience store just a short drive from my office used to sell the biggest and shiniest red apples I had ever set my eyes on. It was always a nice treat to take a break from my work, head down to the store, and buy one of those delicious red apples. One day I walked out of the store with a smile on my face that reflected my pride of ownership. I had just bought a red apple! I couldn't even wait to get back to the office before I sunk my teeth into that juicy red delight. When I did, I was shocked. I had just bitten right into a big brown patch of rotten apple. I spat it out in disgust. It was

---

8   Strong's Concordance, #5273.
9   1 Samuel 16:7, NIV, emphasis added.

such a disappointment. Call me cheap, but I took that apple right back into the store to get my money back.

Everyday life has trained us for the most part to make our appearance look good on the outside. All it takes is showing up to school one day with some unattractive sweater Momma made us wear, and we can be setting ourselves up for some counseling in our adult years. Kids can be ruthless, can't they? As we grow older, we learn how to dress properly for interviews and weddings and other formal occasions. After a while the message sinks in deep: "You are how you look."

In contrast, when Our Heavenly Father views our lives, he is mostly concerned with the inside of our apples. We can be as shiny as a set of loaner tuxedo shoes on the outside, but we cannot fool God. He is looking within. He is looking at our hearts. This can be either good or bad news. It all depends. Do you have a heart of gold or a heart filled with coal? Only God knows the true verdict.

Here is the encouraging news. When we make up our mind to live our lives in such a way that gives God the credit, not us, he determines to reward us in return. If we do everything out of a desire to look good before others and seek their approval, God says that our reward will only be the praise of people.

For the most part when I worked in my dad's warehouse, he was nowhere in sight. He was in his office making calls and paying bills or out on the road seeing his customers. I knew my dad well enough to know what he wanted from me and how he wanted me to perform. It wasn't a mystery because my dad made his standards loud and clear. He especially had that loud thing down to a science!

Likewise, God the Father has made his will for our lives and the work he wants us to perform abundantly clear in his Word. Feed the poor. Comfort the broken. Care for widows and orphans. Heal the sick. Teach his Word to others. The list goes on and on and on. God has made his will overtly unambiguous for us to understand.

The problem is that when we look around, we can't see God with our physical eyes. He's not in the warehouse. So we may think to ourselves: "I need someone to know that I am doing good things down here. I need someone to recognize just how good a person I am!" With a varying degree of pride in our hearts or need of human affirmation, we find ourselves tempted to boast about the good things we have accomplished and the people we have blessed along the way. "Hey, I went down to the soup kitchen to help out yesterday", we may let slip, or "Wish you could have joined me when I helped Granny Jones into her retirement home yesterday."

Jesus says that when our motive for doing good deeds is to be seen by people, then our Father has no reward for us. It would be like me showing up in my dad's office on Friday afternoon to have his secretary Robin punch in the number of hours I worked, and then multiply it by zero. I would be putting my hand out expecting a big stack of five dollar bills coming my way, only to get a high five instead. Believe me, my reaction would not be a happy one. I'd be saying something like, "Now, wait a second! I was working my tail off down there! Where is my pay?"

Jesus teaches us that Our Heavenly Father is not interested in ostentatious religiosity. He does not want us doing good so that we look good on the outside even while our apple is dirty brown on the inside. Even our prayers to God can become a cacophony of noise if our motives are to gain the approval of others. Just listen to what Jesus had to say about how we pray as well as how we perform good deeds:

> And when you pray, do not be like the hypocrites, for they love to pray standing in the synagogues and on the street corners to be seen by others. Truly I tell you, they have received their reward in full. But when you pray, go into your room, close the door and pray to your Father, who is unseen. Then your Father, who sees what is done in secret, will reward you.[10]

It is important for us to remember here that the culture and society to which Jesus was speaking was a highly religious one. Religious people were looked up to as the ones who had it all together. They were the celebrities of Jesus' day. This is in contrast to our own era when religious people are often looked down upon and typecast as being behind-the-times, dated, prudish, and not in touch with reality. Today it takes courage to make a public prayer. It takes courage to let other people know that you are a person of religious faith. A simple prayer before a meal in a restaurant is enough to make some people

10 Matthew 6:5-6

(even Christian folk) feel uncomfortable. We could all benefit from people who are bold enough to pray in public!

So we don't miss the point, let's remember that it all comes back to motives. It comes back to the inside of the apple, not its shade of red or how shiny its skin. God is looking for good fruit to come out of our lives. He is looking for us to do good deeds out of our gratitude for God's kindness, not for human praise and attention.

SHHH ... IT'S A SECRET!

In the above passage, Jesus taught that we are to pray in secret to the Father who is unseen. The Greek word translated here as "secret" is repeated four times in this passage. It means "concealed, private or hidden".[11] Two times it is use to describe our actions. The other two times it is actually used to describe the Father. When Jesus tells us to pray to the Father who is "unseen", he is actually using the word "secret". In other words, pray to the Father who is hidden in secret, and the Father who sees what is done in secret will reward you.

The Bible speaks repeatedly about God being the one who can see what is done in secret. The passages below all use the same word Greek word translated as secret in the above passage:

> *For there is nothing **hidden** that will not be disclosed, and nothing concealed that will not be known or brought out into the open.[12]*

> *This will take place on the day when God judges people's **secrets** through Jesus Christ, as my gospel declares.[13]*

> *Therefore judge nothing before the appointed time; wait until the Lord comes. He will bring to light what is **hidden** in darkness and will expose the motives of the heart. At that time each will receive their praise from God.[14]*

Knowing that the Father is the one who can see everything that is done in secret can either be an alarming or hopeful thought. If we do things in secret that we would not want people to know about, then

11 Strong's Concordance, #2927
12 Luke 8:17, see also Matthew 10:26, Mark 4:22 and Luke 12:2
13 Romans 2:16
14 1 Corinthians 4:5

we may feel like going into hiding from God. But let's be honest with ourselves. We can't hide from God any more than we can from the IRS. They will both eventually find us out. In either case, the result can be quite taxing.

On a more positive note, the idea of God knowing all our secrets is not just related to God's judgment of humanity, although that is positively true. Secrecy with God is actually an invitation to have an intimate relationship with the Father of all creation and Lord of the universe. Think of it this way. Suppose a man and woman have an amazing marriage relationship together. They talk together. They share their innermost secrets with one another, their dreams, hopes, desires, and fears. They are intimate with one another in ways that are exclusive to just the two of them. A good marriage can have a lot of wonderful secret moments, some of which are better left out of the public eye, if you know what I mean!

> *SECRECY WITH GOD IS ACTUALLY AN INVITATION TO HAVE AN INTIMATE RELATIONSHIP WITH THE FATHER OF ALL CREATION AND LORD OF THE UNIVERSE!*

In the same way, God the Father invites us into a secret and intimate relationship with him where we can not only talk to him about every matter in our lives and hear his still, small voice whispering back to us, but we can do things for him that are just between us and him. It's like the man who makes breakfast for his wife in bed first thing in the morning. Or the wife who blesses her husband in ways only she can physically.

Thinking of God in those types of intimate terms may seem unorthodox to say the least. But that is exactly what God the Father desires. He desires a relationship that is so tight, so unifying, and so beautiful that it would not be appropriate for public display. God wants us to share things that are just between us and him in order to draw us closer to one another. Bob Sorge writes:

> The Lord is saying, "I don't want to guide you from a distance. I don't want to have to put a bit in your mouth and jerk you around in order to get your attention and get you on course. I want you to draw close to Me—scootch up close to My

heart—and allow Me to direct your life from a place of intimacy and communion."[15]

And the most amazing promise of all in this passage is that when God sees us praying in secret and helping others without tooting our own horn, he gets all excited and says, "I'm going to bless you back!" How sweet! God is out to reward his people as a lover is out to do good to their mate. He loves us more than we could ever imagine and definitely more than we truly deserve. What an amazing incentive to know that God the Father is out to bless our labors and reward our works of service:

> *Work with enthusiasm, as though you were working for the Lord rather than for people. Remember that the Lord will reward each one of us for the good we do.*[16]

At the end of the day, better yet at the end of our lives, we all want to know that God was pleased with our work here on earth. Jesus promises that if we do our good deeds without fanfare and the hope of gaining the world's praise, we can expect our Father to reward us and say the words every child longs to hear from their father, "Well done!".

Points to Remember:

- Our Good Father wants to reward us for our labors.
- Our Good Father does not want us to do good deeds or pray to look good or for other's approval.
- Secrecy is not about judgment as much as it is about intimacy with God.
- Doing good in secret is a way to develop greater intimacy with Our Good Father.

Prayer:

"Good Father, teach me to do good and to pray only for your approval and not for the approval of man."

---

15 Sorge, Bob. *Secrets of the Secret Place* (Kindle Locations 496-498). Oasis House. Kindle Edition.
16 Ephesians 6:7-8a, NLT

Meditation:

Our Good Father rewards his children.

Group Discussion:

- What do you think of the idea of God wanting to reward you for the good things you do?
- When if ever is it good to tell other people about the good things you have done for God?
- What part of your relationship with God should be kept secret? What part public?

Dig Deeper:

Read through the following verses to study more about God's rewards for your good deeds.

- Matthew 6:5-6: And when you pray, do not be like the hypocrites, for they love to pray standing in the synagogues and on the street corners to be seen by others. Truly I tell you, they have received their reward in full. But when you pray, go into your room, close the door and pray to your Father, who is unseen. Then your Father, who sees what is done in secret, will reward you.
- Ephesians 6:7-8a, NLT: Work with enthusiasm, as though you were working for the Lord rather than for people. Remember that the Lord will reward each one of us for the good we do.
- Colossians 3:23-24: Whatever you do, do your work heartily, as for the Lord rather than for men, knowing that from the Lord you will receive the reward of the inheritance. It is the Lord Christ whom you serve.

CHAPTER FOUR

A Father Who Welcomes Us Home

"Every parent is at some time the father of the unreturned prodigal, with nothing to do but keep his house open to hope."

— JOHN CIARDI

The other day I had an appointment to meet a man from another church for the very first time. He chose the location, a Dunkin Donuts mid-way between our homes and only ten minutes away from each of us. I had never been there, but figured it would be easy enough to find. Unfortunately, the GPS app on my phone was not working properly that morning, so I had to rely on instructions I got off the Internet, an invention I'd thought cutting-edge not so long ago that now seems downright archaic.

The instructions seemed clear. Turn right. Turn left. Then make a final right to my destination. When I took that final right, I began to look for the Dunkin Donuts, but found none in sight. So I kept driving another several miles, got stuck in traffic waiting for a train to pass, then continued going for a few more miles before I finally concluded I had gone too far. By this point, I was fighting off a lot of negative, condemning voices in my mind.

- "You dummy, you should have borrowed your wife's GPS!"
- "You are always making these stupid mistakes. Get your life together!"
- "I can't believe you are so insensitive to others. You should have left much earlier."

What a great way to start a morning! I laid aside my man pride and stopped at a store to ask for directions. The lady behind the counter was just as clueless as I was, but she did make a point to inform me that although I was on the right road, I was in the wrong town. I had definitely overshot my destination. If that wasn't bad enough, I realized I had never exchanged phone numbers with the guy I'd promised to meet, so I had no way of notifying him that I was going to be late. I started composing in my head the apologetic email I would have to send to explain why I had missed our meeting.

Frustrated with myself and feeling like a lost cause for now running fifteen minutes late for a first-time appointment, I hopped back in the car and retraced my route. Five hundred feet before the intersection of my last instructed right turn, I spotted the Dunkin Donuts I had been searching to find. Somehow, I had driven right past the location without even seeing it. I walked tail between my legs, into the Dunkin Donuts, shamed by my own failure and tardiness.

> *WE TRULY LEARN A LOT ABOUT ANOTHER PERSON BY THE WAY THEY RESPOND TO THE FAILURES OF OTHERS.*

"Pierre?" The query came from the man I was planning to meet.

I quickly began to explain. "Yes, it's me. I am so extremely sorry for being late. I totally missed this place as I was driving in."

"No problem," he responded with a gentle and caring voice. "Really, don't worry about it."

I was so grateful for his gracious response. I made sure to ask forgiveness a second and third time during the course of our meeting. But each time I requested his pardon, he was all the more forgiving. This not only humbled me further, it gave me an amazing first impression of a man who extended me such grace. We truly learn a lot about another person by the way they respond to the failures of others.

ONE YOUNG MAN'S FAILURE

Jesus tells a great story about a father's response to a son's utter failure. In this story, we learn a great deal about God and how he responds to our own failures, weaknesses, and sins. Jesus begins:

There was a man who had two sons. The younger one said to his father, 'Father, give me my share of the estate.' So he divided his property between them. Not long after that, the younger son got together all he had, set off for a distant country and there squandered his wealth in wild living.[1]

Let me explain the characters in this story. First you have a father with two sons. The father we can presume is financially successful and secure since he owns an estate. He is not a tyrannical ruler or a control freak. He allows his sons to make good and bad decisions. He even acquiesces to his younger son's request to receive his share of his expected inheritance even before his father's death.

Now this younger son is quite a character. I'd put his age between sixteen and nineteen because that seems to be the time in life when we think we know just about everything there is to know about life and that our parents are totally ignorant. I love this quote ascribed to Mark Twain: "When I was a boy of fourteen, my father was so ignorant I could hardly stand to have the old man around. But when I got to be twenty-one, I was astonished at how much the old man had learned in seven years."[2] [3]

> WHAT TOOK THE FATHER YEARS TO ACCUMULATE, THE SON TOOK ONLY WEEKS TO BLOW. SUCH IS THE NATURE OF LIFE—WHAT TAKES YEARS TO BUILD CAN BE RUINED OVERNIGHT.

The young man in Jesus' story had a pocket full of cash and decided it was time to sow his wild oats. He spared no expense, wasting the entirety of his inheritance in wild living. What had taken the father years to accumulate, the son took no time at all to blow. Such is the nature of life—what takes years to build can be ruined overnight!

Jesus goes on to describe the young man's fate:

After he had spent everything, there was a severe famine in that whole country, and he began to be in need. So he went and hired himself out to a citizen of that country, who sent him to his

---

1   Luke 15:11-13, NIV

2   Some have questioned whether it was truly Twain who made this statement: http://quoteinvestigator.com/2010/10/10/twain-father/, accessed May 24, 2017.

3   http://www.goodreads.com/quotes/78468-when-i-was-a-boy-of-14-my-father-was, accessed May 24, 2017.

fields to feed pigs. He longed to fill his stomach with the pods that the pigs were eating, but no one gave him anything.[4]

We know that Jesus' audience was primarily Jewish. We can safely presume they are imagining the character in this story to be Jewish as well. This is what makes this young Jewish son's actions even more unthinkable. He hires himself into servitude working for a Gentile. If that's not bad enough, his job is to feed the pigs, a creature considered unclean by the Jews. You can just imagine the thoughts of this very religious audience listening to Jesus as they hear this story unfold. "He did what?"

Jesus is not done laying it on thick. He goes on to say that this kid wanted to eat the very food these non-kosher pigs were snorting down. That's when the wayward son hit rock bottom:

When he came to his senses, he said, "How many of my father's hired servants have food to spare, and here I am starving to death! I will set out and go back to my father and say to him: 'Father, I have sinned against heaven and against you. I am no longer worthy to be called your son; make me like one of your hired servants.'"[5]

This young man finally has an awakening. He comes to the realization that his rich dad's own servants were eating better than him. This story reminds me of the one and only time I ran away from home. I was so upset with my mom and dad that I ran all the way down to the end of the block and sat in my friend's tree fort. I wasn't there very long before my stomach began growling. It was at that point I realized I had no money, no job, and that I was a pretty lazy kid. I walked straight back home. My parents had never even realized I had left. What a rebel!

The youth in Jesus' story has now resolved to change and determines to head back home and face up to the error of his ways. The son realizes that he is not only indebted to his father for the wasted finances, but for the shame he has caused his whole family. So he determines not to ask his father for any favors or even the right to be called son, but instead figures he will become one of his father's servants.

---

4   Luke 15:14-16, NIV
5   Luke 15:17-19

If you were to multiply by one hundred my own feelings of shame when I walked into Dunkin' Donuts the other morning, you might come close to the level of shame this young man was feeling as he walked back home with shoulders slumped and head hanging down. He no longer felt worthy to be called son, instead he felt like the most unworthy of servants.

The similarities between this young son and a redeemed child of God are many. Just as the son wasted his father's inheritance, we too have wasted time on sin. Just as he hired himself out to work an undignified job, so we have become slaves to sin in our lives. By God's grace, we too hit that place of desperation where we were famished for something to fill our empty souls. Just as this young son humbled himself and came back to his father, so we humbly returned back to God with penitent hearts. (See Figure 1 at end of chapter).

SINNER SAVED BY GRACE?

The other day, I overheard a Christian guy receiving a compliment. Just as the younger son in the story could only see himself as unworthy, this man did not receive this compliment with gracious appreciation, but insisted: "I am just a sinner saved by grace." To me, his response felt as though he too was seeing himself as that starving vagabond who had returned home only to be a hired worker. The harm in holding such a view of oneself is that it does not coincide with the picture Jesus paints for us of our identity in the Father's mind. Let's look at the contrasting view Jesus gives us of this wayward son:

GROWING UP IN CHURCH, I WAS NEVER TAUGHT ABOUT A GOD WHO GAVE KISSES.

> *So he got up and went to his father. "But while he was still a long way off, his father saw him and was filled with compassion for him; he ran to his son, threw his arms around him and kissed him."*[6]

As mentioned earlier, I grew up going to Sunday school and catechism almost every week. My early religious upbringing portrayed for me a certain view of God. I saw him as an authority figure who meant what he said and said what he meant. If you asked me about God's

---

6   Luke 15:20

emotions, I would say he was probably capable of only one emotion: anger. Joyful, happy, gracious, and loving were not words I would have ever associated with God. Jesus paints us a much different picture of God as Father. In the story, this father gives his son a bear hug and then lays a "wet one" on him. Growing up in church, I was never taught about a God who gave kisses.

This father was so excited to see his son coming from afar that he took off running to meet him on the way. He did not run to greet a sinner saved by grace. He was running to meet his lost son who had come home. What a contrast in view!

How about you? Do you see yourself primarily as a sinner saved by grace or as a child who has come home to your loving and merciful Father?

SOME CULTURAL PERSPECTIVE

Professor of Theology Dr. Kenneth Bailey explains that in Jewish culture of Jesus' day, if a son were to return home after completely wasting his inheritance among Gentiles, the community would likely perform a ceremony called a *kezazah*. In this ceremony, they would break a large pot in front of the wayward traveler and yell, "You are cut off from your people".[7] From that point he would be totally and completely rejected. Bailey suggests that the prodigal son's father in this passage is running to reach his son and offer him welcome and reconciliation before the prodigal can enter the village and be faced with their scorn and rejection of the community.

The image here is of a father risking his own dignity for the sake of saving his son the shame he deserved. Jesus is painting for his audience a picture of God's good news, the gospel. The gospel is God's means of reconciling us as sinful people by taking upon himself all the guilt and shame we so rightly deserve. It is what John Stott calls the self-substitution of God. God took our guilt, shame, and penalty by allowing Jesus to die on the cross for our sins. Jesus is again painting a beautiful picture of our heavenly Father who is completely thrilled to have us come home to him. (See Figure 2 at end of chapter)

---

7 Williams, Matt. "The Prodigal Son's Father Shouldn't Have Run!." Biola Magazine. http://magazine.biola.edu/article/10-summer/the-prodigal-sons-father-shouldnt-have-run/, accessed May 13, 2017.

The son said to him, "Father, I have sinned against heaven and against you. I am no longer worthy to be called your son." But the father said to his servants, "Quick! Bring the best robe and put it on him. Put a ring on his finger and sandals on his feet. Bring the fattened calf and kill it. Let's have a feast and celebrate. For this son of mine was dead and is alive again; he was lost and is found." So they began to celebrate.[8]

Talk about a twist in the story! Perhaps many of us can imagine just what type of wrath we might receive if we came home to our own father after wasting our whole inheritance. We can imagine ourselves being the object of total and utter scorn in our father's eyes. There we are head down, tail between our legs, trudging along back to our dad, hoping to beg for forgiveness. And that is exactly what this young man did.

But the response of this father is nothing less than miraculous. Instead of breaking a pot and rejecting his son, he breaks out with a complete party that spares no expense. Talk about a surprise party! Symbolically, we understand that the robe he put on his son was a means of covering his shame. The ring on his finger was a sign of bestowing his favor and blessing. The new sandals now covered the feet that once walked away from home.

JEALOUS SIBLINGS KNOW HOW TO RUIN A PARTY!

I am the youngest of six kids. Yes, that makes me the baby. My older sisters like to give me a hard time about being pampered all my life by my mom. When I go back home, she makes me all my favorite Lebanese dishes as if I were a king returning from war. My sisters always tease, "Kill the fattened calf; the prodigal son is coming home!" I'm not bothered by it though. Such ridicule comes with the territory of being your mom's favorite child!

The older brother in this story was not so happy about his brother's homecoming. He was coming home from a long day's work when he heard the sound of music and dancing. "What's going on?" he inquired of a servant. The servant explained that his brother had made it back home and his father was throwing a party that would pale in comparison to the brother's own Bar Mitzvah.

---

8 Luke 15:21-24, NIV

The older brother became angry and refused to go in. So his father went out and pleaded with him. But he answered his father, "Look! All these years I've been slaving for you and never disobeyed your orders. Yet you never gave me even a young goat so I could celebrate with my friends. But when this son of yours who has squandered your property with prostitutes comes home, you kill the fattened calf for him!"[9]

Can you hear the indignation in this brother's voice? Here's the irony. He saw himself as a slave in his father's house. He said to his father, "All these years I've been slaving for you." He was doing everything right and yet felt he was not getting even a small reward for his labor. Now this prostitute-purchasing brother comes home, and he gets a full blown party thrown for him. You-have-got-to-be-kidding-me! He is not the least bit happy. His dad tries to calmly explain:

"My son," the father said, "you are always with me, and everything I have is yours. But we had to celebrate and be glad, because this brother of yours was dead and is alive again; he was lost and is found."[10]

WHAT GOES AROUND COMES AROUND

When we are disappointed in life by other people's mistakes, we have two choices. We can treat people with the judgment and rejection that their misdeeds deserve. We can bring up their faults, remind them how badly they have failed, and turn them into a slave trying to earn our forgiveness and forbearance. Or we can take the approach of this father. We can be gracious, kind, forbearing, and forgiving of every wrong. Just be forewarned. Life tends to work in cycles, and whatever we dish out, we often end up having to eat.

Remember the appointment I mentioned earlier to which I showed up unfashionably late? Ironically, **the very next morning** I had an appointment with a longtime friend for breakfast at a local restaurant. I showed up to the restaurant at 6:50. This time I was ten minutes early, thank you very much. But when 7 o'clock came, my friend had still not arrived. Typically, this guy is early, so I was a

9   Luke 15:28-30, NIV
10 Luke 15:31-32, NIV

bit puzzled. After a few minutes, I sent him a text to let him know I had arrived. I waited fifteen minutes, but no friend. I waited another fifteen and still no friend. Figuring he must have forgotten to set his alarm or forgot our meeting, I decided to leave the restaurant. As I left, the waitress remarked, "You got stood up, huh?" The truth hurts.

About ten minutes after leaving the restaurant, I received a call from my friend. Boy, was he apologetic for missing our meeting! I had to stop him mid-sentence. I explained to him what had happened to me just the day before, how I had been fifteen minutes late to a first-time get-together. I told him how gracious this other guy was to me and how I truly understand we all make these kinds of mistakes. "Don't sweat it." I said to him with a great level of confidence and conviction.

You see, I was able to show my friend grace because I myself had already received grace. Do you get that? I was able to extend mercy because I had already received mercy. I knew the shame of being late for an appointment, but also the forgiveness of a kind man. I knew what it was to be remorseful for my errors, but I also knew what it meant to be forgiven and not judged for my mistakes.

Friend, this is the good news with skin on. This is what Jesus came to die for. He came to give himself totally and completely for our mistakes, our errors, our sins in order that you and I could be let off the hook and forgiven by God of all our transgressions. The Lord simply wants us to come back to him, admit we were wrong, accept the penalty Jesus paid for our sins, and then live as a son or daughter of God.

Are you ready to come home to the Father? He is waiting for you with open arms. Pray this prayer with me:

"Heavenly Father, I know that I myself have sinned. I have done things, said things and thought things that were shameful and wrong. I admit, I need your forgiveness. I need your restoration. Thank you for sending Jesus to be my Savior, to die on the cross for my sins and to make me whole again. I now accept Jesus' death on the cross for the payment of my sins and I welcome him into my life. Good Father, this day, I make the choice to come home to you and begin a lifelong friendship together. Amen."

Welcome home!

Points to Remember:

- We learn a lot about a man by the way he responds to the failures of others.
- We see ourselves as sinners saved by grace, but God sees us as sons and daughters.
- The Father has open arms and is ever waiting for us to turn from our sin and come back to him.

Prayer:

"Good Father, I turn from all my sin, my guilt and my shame and I turn my life over to You. I accept your grace."

Meditation:

Father welcomes me home.

Group Discussion:

- Have you ever been let off the hook by someone for a mistake you made? How did it feel?
- What ways could you see an earthly father responding to a child who loses their inheritance?
- Do you tend to see yourself as a "sinner saved by grace" or as a child who has come home?
- What types of sins in the world are the kind you would have the hardest time forgiving?

Dig Deeper:

Read through the following verses to study more the Father who welcomes us home:

- Luke 15:14-16: After he had spent everything, there was a severe famine in that whole country, and he began to be in need. So he went and hired himself out to a citizen of that country, who sent him to his fields to feed pigs. He longed to fill his stomach with the pods that the pigs were eating, but no one gave him anything.
- Luke 15:17-19: When he came to his senses, he said, "How many of my father's hired servants have food to spare, and here I am starving to death! I will set out and go back to my father and say to him: 'Father, I have sinned against heaven and against you. I am no longer worthy to be called your son; make me like one of your hired servants.'"
- John 8:34: Jesus replied, "Very truly I tell you, everyone who sins is a slave to sin."
- Luke 15:20: So he got up and went to his father. But while he was still a long way off, his father saw him and was filled with compassion for him; he ran to his son, threw his arms around him and kissed him.

Figure 1:

The Younger Son	Child of God
The younger son thought he knew a better way to live and wasted his father's inheritance.	**We have wasted time on sin.** "For you have spent enough time in the past doing what pagans choose to do—living in debauchery, lust, drunkenness, orgies, carousing and detestable idolatry" (1 Peter 4:3).
He hired himself out.	**We became slaves to sin.** "Jesus replied, 'Very truly I tell you, everyone who sins is a slave to sin'" (John 8:34).
He longed to fill his stomach, but no one gave him anything.	**We became hungry for something different and could not find fulfillment in the world, an empty, gnawing feeling.**
"I am no longer worthy to be called your son; make me like one of your hired servants."	**We see ourselves as unworthy servants of God.** "I am just a sinner saved by grace."

Figure 2:

The Prodigal's Father	Our Heavenly Father
Was anxious and excited to see his son come home.	"The Lord is not slow in keeping his promise, as some understand slowness. Instead he is patient with you, not wanting anyone to perish, but everyone to come to repentance" (2 Peter 3:9).
The Father was compassionate towards his son, not angry.	"The LORD is compassionate and gracious, slow to anger, abounding in love" (Psalm 103:8).
The Father ran to his son.	"Come near to God and he will come near to you. Wash your hands, you sinners, and purify your hearts, you double-minded" (James 4:8).
The Father was emotional about his son's return home.	"Jerusalem, Jerusalem, you who kill the prophets and stone those sent to you, how often I have longed to gather your children together, as a hen gathers her chicks under her wings, and you were not willing" (Matthew 23:37).

CHAPTER FIVE

A Father Who Accepts Us

"The greatest gift that you can give to others is the gift of unconditional love and acceptance."

— BRIAN TRACY

I typically do not expect God to speak to us when we enter a McDonald's restroom, but that is exactly what happened to me just the other day. Now I can imagine you are eager to hear how the bathroom of America's most famous fast-food chain became a sanctuary for me, but I first must give you the back story.

A couple of weeks prior to my encounter with God in the bathroom, our church had an outreach at a local Laundromat. We partnered with the owner for a "Grand Re-Opening" where we provided free laundry, games for kids, a bounce house, food and the offer to pray for people. While we were there ministering, I befriended a man who we'll call Bob, and found out that he was recently evicted from his apartment and now homeless.

Bob was not your stereotypical homeless man by any means. He was an intelligent, articulate, sound minded man who truly loved God and had deep spiritual passion and moral convictions. Hard times play no favorites. I felt bad not being able to help Bob in a more practical way than just providing a listening ear, free food and some prayer. When I left the outreach that day to go home, I knew Bob would not have a place to call home that night.

Fast forward a few weeks and I found myself in the same neighborhood going to my dentist for a regularly scheduled teeth cleaning. As I pulled in, I noticed Bob again outside the Laundromat picking up trash, not for the purpose of salvaging his findings, but just to clean up the area. Again, I reiterate, Bob is not your ordinary homeless guy.

I saw him from across the street and yelled out to him, "Hey Bob, it's me, Pastor Pierre" with a friendly wave in his direction. I had to quickly go into the dentist appointment so I asked a somewhat rhetorical question, "Will you be here when I get out?" He nodded in the affirmative and I went to go find my place in the dentist's chair.

I came out of my dentist appointment and sure enough, there was Bob across the street. So I drove over to see him and offered him breakfast at McDonalds. He accepted my offer, but was unwilling to come into my car to ride to the restaurant. He felt that he was too dirty.

I had no problem with him sitting in my car, but I also wanted to honor his sense of dignity and his request to walk. We both left the parking lot, I in my car, Bob on foot, and headed to the McDonald's restaurant located just down the road from the Laundromat parking lot. As I pulled into the parking lot, I saw Bob walking up to the restaurant.

When I got out of my car to go inside, Bob was nowhere in sight. I looked in the restaurant and again, no Bob. Finally, after a few minutes, he popped out of the restaurant's bathroom where he was diligently cleaning his hands before he came out to shake my own. We ordered our food at the counter and while we were waiting for the Egg McMuffins and hash browns to be ready, I decided to use the bathroom myself.

> *IT WAS AS IF GOD THE FATHER WAS USING KATY PERRY TO REMIND ME OF HIS UNCONDITIONAL LOVE FOR ME RIGHT THERE IN THE BATHROOM OF MCDONALDS.*

I walked into the men's restroom pretty unassumingly. Little did I know that I was about to have an encounter with God. As I entered into the bathroom, the melodic sounds from the overhead speakers caught my attention. The song playing throughout the bathroom was unfamiliar to me, but it was surprisingly warm and inviting. The female vocalist beautifully sang of an unconditional love for her lover.

The days when I could name every Top 20 artist, song and sing the lyrics without a second thought have long been over. My Christian contemporary culture of worship, praise and rock music has slowly taken over the jukebox of my mind. So I did what every modern day man would do, I pulled out my Smartphone. "Hey Siri, what's this song?" Momentarily my portable genie in a case responded, "I think it's Unconditionally by Katy Perry". I made a mental note of the song title and artist so I could listen to it later and look up the lyrics online.

In the meantime, as I washed my hands in the McDonald's bathroom, I listened to the words of this love-drenched song drip down like honey from the speakers. It was as if God the Father was using Katy Perry to remind me of his unconditional love for me right there in the bathroom of McDonalds. I felt like God was singing this song over my life and pouring out his love upon me.

Here are some of the lyrics of the song that gripped my heart that morning in McDonalds:

Oh no, did I get too close?
Oh, did I almost see what's really on the inside?
All your insecurities
All the dirty laundry
Never made me blink one time
Unconditional, unconditionally
I will love you unconditionally
There is no fear now
Let go and just be free
I will love you unconditionally[1]

I walked out of that bathroom feeling charged and energized by the song as it reminded me of the unconditional love of the Father who accepts us fully where we are in life. With these thoughts in mind, I departed from the bathroom to meet with Bob for our breakfast together.

I carried our tray and walked over to a table. I sat down and Bob stood. I invited him to sit, but he declined. I began to engage him in dialogue, but before I went very far he interrupted me to excuse himself for his dirty clothes and untidy appearance. He was clearly ashamed of how he looked and concerned with how he smelled. Here was a

---

1   "Unconditionally", Prism, Capital Records, October 2013.

man who had lost his sense of value and who wore not just unwashed clothes, but the shame of feeling dirty and unworthy.

Truth be told, he did look grungy, dirty and unkempt. His hair was messy. His beard was well overgrown and his clothes were visibly dirty. From his appearance anyone in the world could easily judge this man unfavorably. Yet I knew that there was more to Bob than his external appearance. Inside was a real person, a person who God loved unconditionally. Sensing Bob's inner shame, but wanting to help him know that I was not condemning or judging him based on how he looked, I boldly spoke words of affirmation to his heart.

> *Bob, you are a child of God. Your identity is in Christ, not the clothes you wear. I do not see you based on how you are dressed, but based on the type of man I know you are inside. Your identity as a child of God is so much more valuable than your current circumstances. God sees you as complete, clean and whole...and so do I.*

I was looking Bob directly in his eyes and he into mine as I confidently spoke these words of love and affirmation to his soul. Bob nodded his head in acceptance of the higher truth of his identity in Christ which he already knew, but needed to be reminded of in this time of desperation. Or as Katy Perry puts it, "All your insecurities...All the dirty laundry...Never made me blink one time."

THE FATHER'S ACCEPTANCE

No matter how many times we hear the words "God loves you", there can be that question in our hearts, "Does he *really* love me?" We do not need any more superficial spirituality. Like people who ask, "How are you?" as they walk in the opposite direction. No, we need to know whether God loves us in the real sense of seeing us how we are inside and out and totally accepting us in that place. Does God love us when our clothes are dirty, our hair is a mess and more importantly when our hearts are impure by the stains of sin and the associated residue of guilt and shame? That's when we need to know he still loves us.

Is God's love truly unconditional? Or does he just love us when we are on our best behavior before him? Are there any strings attached to the love of God in Christ?

THE FATHER SON RELATIONSHIP

Eric Clapton wrote, sung and produced an award winning song entitled, "My Father's Eyes". Clapton never met his biological father. The lyrics of his song convey the message of how important it is in the crucial moments of our lives to be able to "look into my Father's eyes". As you look into the eyes of your Heavenly Father, what type of eyes look back at you? Are they accepting? Scornful? Angry? Judgemental? How do you imagine the Father looks upon you?

The life of Jesus and his relationship with the Father gives us great hope. Before Jesus ever appeared on the public scene of ministry, we see how the Father blesses him and shows his Son the unconditional love and acceptance we all long to know for ourselves. The stage is set in "Bethany beyond Jordan", where John the Baptist was baptizing penitent sinners.

John was a pretty wild looking character himself. He likely resembled my friend Bob or a hippie musician more than he did a modern day television preacher. "John's clothes were made of camel's hair, and he had a leather belt around his waist. His food was locusts and wild honey."[2] John was not looking to win any popularity contests for his choice of clothing, his dietary selection or the smell of his locust laden breath. His message was no more popular either. He called the religious people of his day a "brood of vipers" and his message to the general population could be summarized in one word —repent![3]

IT WOULD MAKE MORE SENSE FOR JOHN TO REPENT OF HIS SINS AND BE BAPTIZED BY JESUS THAN THE REVERSE.

John's mission was to prepare the people for someone greater than himself – the coming Messiah. He forewarned the people that someone was about to come on the scene who was more powerful than he and who was worthy of greater honor. If you have ever been around a fire and brimstone preacher, you know how their words have a way of cutting down deep and bringing great conviction of sin. It is in this type of intense and hot spiritual atmosphere where our story unfolds.

---

2   Matthew 3:4
3   Matthew 3:2,7

Then Jesus came from Galilee to the Jordan to be baptized by John. But John tried to deter him, saying, "I need to be baptized by you, and do you come to me?" Jesus replied, "Let it be so now; it is proper for us to do this to fulfill all righteousness." Then John consented. As soon as Jesus was baptized, he went up out of the water. At that moment heaven was opened, and he saw the Spirit of God descending like a dove and alighting on him.[4]

John the Baptist obviously had some level of revelation into the person of Jesus. His words, "I need to be baptized by you" indicate that John recognized the superiority of his younger cousin Jesus. The one John had prophesied would come was now in his midst. John immediately discerned that the righteousness of Jesus exceeded his own. It would make more sense for John to repent of his sins and be baptized by Jesus than the reverse.

Jesus acknowledged this truth as well, but he told John to proceed with the baptism. Jesus explained that this was being done to fulfill the Father's purposes for Jesus' life and ministry, not because John was worthy to perform the task. In obedience, John acquiesced to the Savior's request, and that is when things really start to get exciting! As Jesus comes out of the baptismal waters of the Jordan, the heavens open and the Spirit of God descends upon Jesus, not in the form of a dove, but gracefully and peacefully like one.

> THE FATHER THROUGH THE SPIRIT REVEALS THE IDENTITY OF JESUS TO EVERYONE WITHIN EAR SHOT.

It is now one of those rare moments in Scripture where we are about to witness every member of the Trinity, Father, Son and Holy Spirit, all in one place on earth. When a special moment like this occurs, you better brace yourself for something spectacular to happen! The Father through the Spirit reveals the identity of Jesus to everyone within ear shot. "And a voice from heaven said, 'This is my Son, whom I love; with him I am well pleased.'"[5]

---

4   Matthew 3:13-16
5   Matthew 3:17

THE FATHER'S BLESSING

The first blessing of the Father is to identify Jesus as his Son. Jesus is not just a prophet. He is not just a good moral teacher. He is not just a philosopher or philanthropist. He is not just a religious leader. Jesus is God's very own Son! Talk about an introduction! It would be one thing for me to make a self-declaration of being part of God's family. "Hi, my name is Pierre. I am a child of God." It would be a whole different story if the heavens broke open and God spoke audibly, "Pierre is my son!" Now that would get people's attention, including my own!

But Jesus was no ordinary son. I mean, after all, you can have good sons, bad sons, shameful sons and sons that make you proud. So what type of son is Jesus? He is the son that God loves! Some Bibles translate this phrase to read that Jesus is God's "beloved Son".

JESUS IS COMPLETELY ACCEPTED IN THE FATHER'S EYES.

Now we are learning not only about Jesus' identity, but also about his relationship with the Father — it is a relationship built on love!

Last and definitely not least, Father speaks these amazing words about Jesus, his beloved Son, "I am pleased with him". This last expression of affection and affirmation is like the crown upon the head of a king. Father not only loves Jesus, he is 100% pleased with him as a person. He is satisfied with Jesus. Jesus is enough. Jesus is completely accepted in the Father's eyes.

What makes this statement all the more remarkable is that it comes before Jesus begins his public ministry! How many sick people had Jesus healed up until now? None. How many demons had Jesus already cast out by this point in his life? None. How many pitchers of water have been turned into wine? Zero. And yet, Father God says of Jesus, "I am completely satisfied with my beloved Son!" Our accomplishments are not what make us whole. What makes us whole is the Father's love.

OUR ACCOMPLISHMENTS ARE NOT WHAT MAKE US WHOLE. WHAT MAKES US WHOLE IS THE FATHER'S LOVE.

The timing of these words is not only significant because they occurred before Jesus performed any great works, they are also important because of what happened immediately after the baptism. "Then Jesus was led by the Spirit into the wilderness to be tempted by the devil."[6] The application for our own lives is vitally important as well. We will have greater victory over temptation if we focus on our identity in Christ rather than our shortcomings.

The next time Jesus would hear these same words of affirmation and approval from the Father would come on the Mount of Transfiguration.[7] It was at this moment when Jesus was being glorified before his closest friends and disciples, undoubtedly a highlight of his time on earth. Thankfully, the Father spoke these words to Jesus before this moment. So we know that his approval and acceptance was not based on Jesus' performance, but on the Father's love.

> WE WILL HAVE GREATER VICTORY OVER TEMPTATION IF WE FOCUS ON OUR IDENTITY IN CHRIST RATHER THAN OUR SHORTCOMINGS.

RESEARCH SHOWS OUR NEED OF ACCEPTANCE

Over forty years of research with thousands of people from different cultures worldwide has revealed that the perceived acceptance or rejection of one's parents, and in particular the father or male figure, has profound implications for a person's future. A child who perceives they are rejected by their parents, and especially their father, can have issues in adulthood with psychological adjustment, depression, anxiety, insecurity, behavioral problems and substance abuse.[8]

Furthermore, a person who experiences parental rejection in childhood is more likely to develop a worldview that deems God and the supernatural in a negative, judgmental, harsh and critical light. In fact, societies where children tend to be rejected culturally usually portray God and the supernatural as being malevolent, not benevolent.[9]

---

6   Matthew 4:1

7   Matthew 17:5, Mark 9:7, Luke 9:35

8   Journal of the Society for Psychological Anthropology, Parental Acceptance-Rejection: Theory, Methods, Cross-Cultural Evidence, and Implications, Volume 33, Issue 3, September 2005, Pages 299-334, Ronald P. Rohner, Abdul Khaleque, David E. Cournoyer

9   Ibid., 318

This news may not sound very uplifting, especially if you were raised in a hostile environment, or one in which your parents and particularly your father showed you rejection instead of unconditional love and acceptance. You may have been raised in an environment where there was not even a paternal figure present. Or you had a father figure, but always felt like his acceptance of you was based on what you did (performance), not who you were as a person (identity). In any and all cases, there is hope.

Research has also shown that not all people who had a negatively perceived upbringing are necessarily subjected to the associated issues in adulthood. The determining factor of whether a person can overcome is based on one's belief they can "exert at least a modicum of control over what happens to them" and do not feel like helpless "pawns".[10]

WE MUST EACH MAKE THE CHOICE TO NOT SEE OURSELVES AS VICTIMS OF THE PAST, BUT INSTEAD AS VICTORIOUS THROUGH JESUS CHRIST OUR LORD.

Therefore, how we respond to our childhood upbringing is vitally important. As children of a loving and good heavenly Father, we have the power and ability to overcome even the worst of childhood upbringings if we truly believe in the unconditional love and acceptance of God the Father. We must each make the choice to not see ourselves as victims of the past, but instead as victorious through Jesus Christ our Lord.

FATHER'S ACCEPTANCE OF JESUS AND YOU

"But wait a moment", you might ask, "What does the Father's acceptance of Jesus have to do with me?" We may understand that the Father accepted Jesus unconditionally even before he performed any miracles, but how do we know that we too are accepted fully in his love?

The answer lies within our identity "in Christ". When you accepted Jesus into your life as your Lord and Savior, you received a completely new identity. "This means that anyone who belongs to Christ has

---

10 Journal of the Society for Psychological Anthropology, Parental Acceptance-Rejection: Theory, Methods, Cross-Cultural Evidence, and Implications, Volume 33, Issue 3, September 2005, Page 315, Ronald P. Rohner, Abdul Khaleque, David E. Cournoyer

become a new person. The old life is gone; a new life has begun!"[11] The day that you said, "Jesus, my life is yours" God heard that request and chose at that moment to no longer see you based on your faults and transgressions, but to see you as he sees his son Jesus – completely accepted and beloved.

The day I met with Bob in McDonald's I offered him two things. I invited him to join me as a guest at the local gym down the road so he could take a shower and clean himself up. I also offered him some new clothing so he could change out of his dirty garb and feel refreshed. In Christ, the same is true for you and me. When we accept Jesus as our Savior and Lord, God cleanses us from all our sins and clothes us with his "robes of righteousness."[12]

> AS WE LEAVE THE WATERS OF BAPTISM, THE SAME VOICE FROM HEAVEN SPEAKS OVER OUR LIVES SAYING TO US, "THIS IS MY CHILD, IN WHOM I AM WELL PLEASED!".

Furthermore, Paul explains that in the waters of baptism, we are baptized "into Christ" and come out clothed a new man or woman. "So in Christ Jesus you are all children of God through faith, for all of you who were baptized into Christ have clothed yourselves with Christ."[13] As we leave the waters of baptism, the same voice from heaven speaks over our lives saying to us, "This is my child, in whom I am well pleased!" Praise be to God our Father!

No longer do we need to work and strive for the Father's approval! No longer do we need to jump through the religious hoops of performance-oriented life and Christianity. We can throw out all the lies we have been told or told ourselves such as:

"If I could just stop this one pervasive sin in my life, then God would love me."

"If I read my Bible more frequently, then God would really love me."

"If I just prayed enough God will love me."

"If I prayed *and* fasted, then God would *really* love me."

---

11 2 Corinthians 5:17, NLT
12 Isaiah 61:10
13 Galatians 3:26, 27

"Beloved" Child of God

Father's love

What does God say about me? → accordance or write down

identity is crisis Apple of my eye Righteousness of Christ

"If I...." You can fill in the blank. What is it that you have believed you need to do in order to be loved and accepted by the Father? If it is not the religious hoops we try to jump through, it is the "hoops of righteousness" that have been placed before us by our parents and particularly our fathers. If I get good enough grades, then my parents will accept me. If I do well in sports, then my dad will love me. If I get into the best schools, land the right type of job or enter into the right profession, then my dad will approve of me.

> **IN CHRIST, THE FATHER HAS ALREADY APPROVED OF US. WE ARE ACCEPTED. WE ARE LOVED.**

In Christ, the Father has already approved of us. We are accepted. We are loved. We are cherished for who we are today, not just for who we will become some day in the future. Paul wrote to the church in Ephesus explaining to them the great riches of their identity in Christ.

> *Blessed be the God and Father of our Lord Jesus Christ, who has blessed us with all spiritual blessings in heavenly places in Christ: According as he has chosen us in him before the foundation of the world, that we should be holy and without blame before him in love: Having predestinated us to the adoption of children by Jesus Christ to himself, according to the good pleasure of his will, to the praise of the glory of his grace, wherein he has made us accepted in the beloved, in whom we have redemption through his blood, the forgiveness of sins, according to the riches of his grace.[14]*

God has adopted us as children through his son Jesus Christ. As a result, we are fully accepted in his sight, members of his family, and beloved children of God who are completely forgiven and free of all guilt, shame and condemnation. Now that is some very good news!

STOP LIVING IN A CEMENT HOUSE!

God has made the decision to see you as completely accepted and loved in Christ. His decision is final and it is complete. Yet, the truth of God's unconditional love is not enough to change us. We must also agree with the truth of his love and reject the lies that we keep telling

---

14 Ephesians 1:3-7, American King James Version

ourselves about our identity. We must believe the truth, "I am loved and accepted by God" above all other lies or even "lesser truths" that have penetrated our hearts and minds.

Many of us have been programmed to believe things about ourselves that are no longer true in Christ. And unfortunately, many of the beliefs we have held about ourselves have been taught to us in church and through our religious catechism. We have been programmed to believe "I am a sinner" instead of believing "I am a beloved child of God."

Truth be told, we still all struggle with sin. If our identity were based on our performance alone, the statement "I am a sinner", would be completely true. Yet, there is a higher and greater truth about who we are in Christ that I would like to explain through an analogy.

In my home I have an unfinished basement. Now let's imagine that you were going to visit my house for the first time. Before getting there, you were blindfolded, driven to my home and then led down into the basement before seeing any other part of my home – the exterior, the foyer, the kitchen, etc. You are now standing in my basement and the blindfolds are removed from your eyes. What do you see?

You see the cement walls of my unfinished basement. So based on the knowledge you have, you believe that my house is made of cement. The blindfolds go back on, you are kindly escorted from my home and asked the simple question, "What is Pierre's house made of?" You respond based only on what you have seen. "Pierre lives in a cement house." Now that does not sound so appealing, does it?

ARE YOU FOCUSED ON THE BASEMENT OF YOUR PAST LIFE BEFORE CHRIST OR ON YOUR NEW IDENTITY IN CHRIST?

But here is the higher truth. If you were to see the outside of my home, you would realize that it is not really made of cement. It is actually sided with cedar wood. It is not unpainted and unfurnished like my basement; it is painted and fully furnished. My home is a beautiful gift from God to me and my family. Thank you, Lord!

In the same way, many of us are so focused on who we are in ourselves that we have not stepped back to see and recognize the beautiful identity we have from God in Christ. The basement of our lives says "We are sinners." And to some degree, this is true. Yet, the greater and higher truth is that in Christ we are complete and whole. It is a matter of focus. Are you focused on the basement of your past life before Christ or on your new identity in Christ?

> Consequently, **you are no longer** foreigners and strangers, but fellow citizens with God's people and also members of his household, built on the foundation of the apostles and prophets, with Christ Jesus himself as the chief cornerstone. In him the whole building is joined together and rises to become a holy temple in the Lord. And in him you too are being built together to become a dwelling in which God lives by his Spirit.[15]

"See what great love the Father has lavished on us, that we should be called children of God! And that is what we are!"[16] Child of God, take hold of the truth of what God says about you in Christ and repeat and rehearse these words over and over again until they are embedded into your soul like the words of a popular song that you just can't get out of your head. "I am unconditionally loved and accepted by God."

Points to Remember:

- Our Good Father loves and accepts us unconditionally because of Christ.
- Our accomplishments are not what make us whole. What makes us whole is the Father's love.
- Because of Christ, Our Good Father sees us as his beloved children, not as wretched sinners.

Prayer:

"Good Father, thank you for making me your beloved child in whom you are well pleased."

Meditation:

"I am unconditionally loved and accepted by God."

---

15 Ephesians 2:19-21, bold and italics added
16 1 John 3:1a

Group Discussion:

- On a scale of 1 to 10, how would you rate your perception of paternal acceptance as a child? (1 being the lowest and 10 the highest)
- How would you complete this sentence? "More often than not, I see myself as _____ in the eyes of God.
- How might focusing on your identity in Christ instead of your performance change the way you live?

Dig Deeper:

Read through the following verses to study more about God's unconditional acceptance.

- Then Jesus came from Galilee to the Jordan to be baptized by John. But John tried to deter him, saying, "I need to be baptized by you, and do you come to me?" Jesus replied, "Let it be so now; it is proper for us to do this to fulfill all righteousness." Then John consented. As soon as Jesus was baptized, he went up out of the water. At that moment heaven was opened, and he saw the Spirit of God descending like a dove and alighting on him." (Matthew 3:13-16)
- Blessed be the God and Father of our Lord Jesus Christ, who has blessed us with all spiritual blessings in heavenly places in Christ: According as he has chosen us in him before the foundation of the world, that we should be holy and without blame before him in love: Having predestinated us to the adoption of children by Jesus Christ to himself, according to the good pleasure of his will, to the praise of the glory of his grace, wherein he has made us accepted in the beloved. In whom we have redemption through his blood, the forgiveness of sins, according to the riches of his grace. (Ephesians 1:3-7, American King James Version)
- Consequently, you are no longer foreigners and strangers, but fellow citizens with God's people and also members of his household, built on the foundation of the apostles and prophets, with Christ Jesus himself as the chief cornerstone. In him the whole building is joined together and rises to become a holy temple in the Lord. And in him you too are being built together to become a dwelling in which God lives by his Spirit. (Ephesians 2:19-21)

CHAPTER SIX

A Father Who Heals Us

"Come, and see the victories of the cross. Christ's wounds are thy healings, His agonies thy repose, His conflicts thy conquests, His groans thy songs, His pains thine ease, His shame thy glory, His death thy life, His sufferings thy salvation."

— MATTHEW HENRY

I could not stop crying. I was kneeling and weeping at the altar rail of a church that I had never before visited, a total emotional wreck. The tears were not just trickling down my face; it was an utter downpour. As the tears were pouring out of my eyes, my nose was running like an open, unrestrained faucet. While I looked like a complete mess from the outside, I felt an all-consuming powerful blanket of warmth and love surrounding me like I had never experienced.

Just moments prior I was sitting in a pew listening intently and without any great emotion to an eloquent, soft-spoken message on the healing power of the cross. I had agreed to attend a weekend conference on the topic of emotional healing with a friend. I was going along for the ride thinking that it would be a great way to support my friend, but I personally did not feel I had any need for healing myself. Truth be told, I came somewhat guarded and cautious about being in an environment where I feared emotionalism, self-pity and blaming others could take an unhealthy priority over rationalism, intellect and human willpower.

My intellectual defenses and pride were gracefully disarmed not only by the speaker's words that were biblically sound, but by his humble delivery of the message of the cross. As I listened to this intelligent and gentle hearted man speak, the cognitive hurdles I had towards the topic of inner healing were not only being leaped over, they were completely knocked down.

No longer obstructed behind those mental barriers, my heart laid bare - open for the Great Physician to do his best work of healing me from the inside out. When the speaker gave an invitation for prayer, I made a willful, rational and intuitive decision to respond to what I believed to be a phenomenal, thought-provoking biblically grounded message. I had only planned to spend a quiet moment or two in prayer talking to God about what I had just heard. Yet once I got just a few feet away from the altar, an outpouring of God's love drenched me unexpectedly.

As I knelt there by the altar, vulnerable and raw, with more external emotions being expressed than any man would ever want to do in public, or even private for that matter, a gentle hand was laid upon my shoulder. One of the ministers of the church was there to comfort me and graciously provide tissue after tissue to help me clean up after the tsunami of tears now gushing out of my eyes.

Eventually, the rate of the tears began to slow down and I started to catch my breath. The minister then asked me in a gentle voice, "What is the Lord doing in your heart right now?" I wish that I had a profound answer in response, but quite honestly, I had no idea what the Lord was doing! I just knew that I was being healed from within. My three-word response, "I don't know", only led to another wave of deep weeping and mourning that poured out of me.

In the midst of what the world would describe as an unmanly moment, my whole body was enveloped in the unconditional love of God. A situation like this could easily bring a boatload of guilt and shame upon any man who ever believed the lie that "Real Men Don't Cry". And yet, I felt nothing but love – the pure, unadulterated, supernatural love of my Good Father. I appreciate Jack Frost's description of his encounter with the Father's love at a pastor's conference as it in so many ways describes my own experience.

The presence of God's compassion and acceptance fell on me immediately. I did not understand what was happening, but it felt as if hot, liquid love was pouring into my soul. I began crying like a baby as I lay on the floor. Such displays of emotion were not normal for me. I always had every emotion in check, especially in front of my wife, children, or other ministers. But my mask was off now. I was completely undone.[1]

WE ALL NEED HEALING

I had already come to grips with the fact that I needed forgiveness in my life. Only a few years prior to this experience, I had first come to know Jesus as my Savior and was happily walking and growing in the new and wonderful life that Christ had offered me. I understood the fact that I had sinned and needed forgiveness. That became quite evident to me. Now on this day, I was realizing that not only was Jesus my Savior, he was my healer.

> JESUS CAME NOT ONLY TO FORGIVE OUR SINS, BUT TO BRING HEALING TO THE PAIN WE EXPERIENCE THROUGH THE SINS OF OTHERS.

Jesus came not only to forgive our sins, but to bring healing to the pain we experience through the sins of others.

I grew up with what I still perceive to this day to be a fairly normal upbringing. I did not experience any major traumatic rejection or abuse as a child. My parents were not divorced. I was never verbally, physically or sexually abused. I played sports, went to school, dated, had fun and lived a generally positive life through my early twenties when I had this encounter.

Of course, there were hurtful events that occurred in my life, like the insensitive words spoken by peers, the common rejections each of us faces along the way in life, not to mention the pain that my entire family felt as a result of the drug and alcohol addictions of my oldest brother. (I am grateful to God that my brother experienced a radical transformation by the power of God and became one of the primary reasons I came to faith myself. Thank you, Good Father!)

Somehow, up until this point in my life, I had done a fairly good job at covering over these hurts like a breastplate of armor over my chest. I had

1   Frost, Jack. Experiencing Father's Embrace (p. 28). Destiny Image. Kindle Edition.

learned how to cope with the pain of this world and function normally without regard to the chinks in my armor. Now in one full sweep, it was as if the Lord was reaching into my heart and healing every past hurt and pain that I had so conveniently tucked away under the veneer of having it all together. Who was I kidding? We all need healing.

In his book, *Healing for Damaged Emotions*, David A. Seamands explains the common need for healing we all have in life through an illustration in nature.

> In most of the parks, the naturalists can show you a cross section of a great tree they have cut, and they will point out that the rings of the tree reveal the developmental history, year by year. Here's a ring that represents a year when there was a terrible drought. Here are a couple of rings from years when there was too much rain. Here's where the tree was struck by lightning. Here are some normal years of growth. This ring shows a forest fire that almost destroyed the tree. Here's another of savage blight and disease. All of this lies embedded in the heart of the tree, representing the autobiography of its growth. That's the way it is with us. Just a few thin layers beneath the protective bark— the concealing, protective mask— are the recorded rings of our lives. There are scars of ancient, painful hurts ... as when a little boy rushed downstairs one Christmas dawn and discovered in his Christmas stocking a dirty old rock, put there to punish him for some trivial boyhood naughtiness. This scar has eaten away at him, causing all kinds of interpersonal difficulties.[2]

WE ALL NEED HEALING.

If your life up until now were sliced open like a tree in the forest, what would you find in the rings? For some, the damage may be minor and the evidence of a healthy past can be seen by the vitality of their present flourishing life. At the other extreme, some people would have a hard time identifying very many rings in the trees of their life without

IF SOMEONE TOOK A CROSS-SECTION OF YOUR TREE OF LIFE, HOW WOULD IT LOOK ON THE INSIDE?

2   Seamands, David A.. Healing for Damaged Emotions (p. 13). David C. Cook. Kindle Edition.

significant blight and damage. How about you? If someone took a cross-section of your tree of life, how would it look on the inside?

THE POWER OF THREE WORDS

Hurt, pain and rejection were not foreign concepts to the Son of God. In fact, the Bible plainly states that Jesus came to his own people and yet, "his own did not receive him".[3] Speaking of the coming Messiah, Isaiah forecasted the rejection of Jesus centuries before his arrival on the scene.

THE ENTIRE NARRATIVE OF ALL HUMAN HISTORY COULD HAVE CHANGED IN THAT ONE MOMENT IF JESUS CHOSE THREE DIFFERENT WORDS.

"He was despised and rejected by mankind, a man of suffering, and familiar with pain. Like one from whom people hide their faces he was despised, and we held him in low esteem."[4] Not only did Jesus receive the personal rejection of many he encountered, he came to bear the hurt and pain suffered by all of humanity. Isaiah continues in the following verses:

Surely he took up our pain and bore our suffering, yet we considered him punished by God, stricken by him, and afflicted. But he was pierced for our transgressions, he was crushed for our iniquities; the punishment that brought us peace was on him, and by his wounds we are healed.[5]

Jesus, the Son of God, came to earth to bear the full weight of sin on his shoulders. He came not only so we could be forgiven of our sins, but so that we could receive the full redemption of healing that flows from the Father's heart of love to his children.

As Christ was being mocked, scorned and crucified next to two criminals, he offered up a humble prayer to the Father. "Jesus said, 'Father, forgive them, for they do not know what they are doing."[6] "Father, forgive them", three simple but profound words Jesus spoke changed history forever. With these three words, the floodgates of healing from heaven were opened for all humanity to experience the

---

3   John 1:11
4   Isaiah 53:3
5   Isaiah 53:4,5
6   Luke 23:34

Father's love and grace. The entire narrative of all human history could have changed in that one moment if Jesus chose three different words.

"Father, scorn them."

"Father, get them."

"Father, punish them."

"Father, show them."

"Father, crucify them."

If we were honest, many of us would have to agree that under the same set of unjust circumstances that Jesus faced, our gut prayer would **not** be, "Father, forgive them." It would be more like, "Father, bring judgment!" or "Father, get revenge!" or maybe, "Father, punish them!" And yet amidst a vocabulary full of choices, Jesus selected these words, "Father, forgive them." Talk about amazing grace!

THE HEALING HEART OF GOD

As explained at the start of our journey together, Jesus came to reveal the heart of the Father. He came to show us what the Father is really like and how the Father would really respond to humanity's frailties and failures. Throughout the life of Jesus, we see a common theme of healing and redemption. The Father's heart for all humanity is not for our destruction, but for our healing and restoration. Our Good Father sent Jesus as his delegate to release his healing into our brokenness.

OUR GOOD FATHER SENT JESUS AS HIS DELEGATE TO RELEASE HIS HEALING INTO OUR BROKENNESS.

As we read through the Gospels, we see one account after another of Jesus extending the grace and healing of God to humanity. Along with the provision of healing, Jesus had to teach his disciples time and again that the nature and heart of God the Father is not for people's destruction or annihilation, but their redemption and salvation.

Two of Jesus' closest companions, James and John, had a less gracious response when they experienced the rejection of their Messiah. Jesus had sent messengers ahead of him to find sleeping accommodation in a Samaritan village, "but the people there did not welcome him, because he was heading for Jerusalem." When the disciples James and John saw this, they asked, 'Lord, do you want us to call fire down from heaven to destroy them?'"[7]

Nobody was going to pull one over on these guys. James and John were ready to wield their spiritual powers to deep fry an entire city with God's judgment! The revelation of the goodness and mercy of God the Father as taught by Jesus had not yet saturated the minds of these future all-stars in the faith. Instead of encouraging further destruction, Jesus rebuked his disciples. James and John missed it. And so did Peter.

At the time of Jesus' greatest betrayal, he was turned in by Judas Iscariot and surrounded by a group of armed men. Simon Peter, in an act of retaliation, pulled out a sword and sliced off the ear of Malchus, the servant of the high priest. It could be easy to justify the indignation felt by Peter and even respect his desire to defend the Lord. We all want friends who will stick up for us and fight our cause, right?

> JESUS WAS MORE CONCERNED WITH HEALING AND SALVATION THAN HE WAS SELF-PRESERVATION.

Yet Jesus, the one being betrayed, not only condemned such retaliatory measures, he extended his hand and healed Malchus' ear. You just have to wonder how this physical healing may have opened Malchus' spiritual ears to the person and message of Jesus. Amazingly, Jesus was more concerned with the healing and salvation of others than in his own self-preservation.

After the ascension of Jesus and the outpouring of God's Spirit, the original disciples came to understand the nature of God to forgive, not to condemn. Stephen, the first martyred apostle, emulated the forgiving nature of his Savior even at the moment of his death. "While they were stoning him, Stephen prayed, 'Lord Jesus, receive my spirit.' Then he fell on his knees and cried out, 'Lord, do not hold this sin against them.' When he had said this, he fell asleep."[8]

Stephen not only forgave those who killed him, he sought for God to show them mercy. A subtle but important distinction exists between

7   Luke 9:53-54
8   Acts 7:59-60

our forgiving of others and furthermore wanting God to forgive them as well. At times we can muster up the ability to forgive others, but we want them to still be on the hook with God. We forgive, but we hope, expect and may even ask for God to judge. "I forgive them, Lord. Now you go after them." If we examined our hearts, we would realize that, at times, we actually hope for a worse outcome for the people we "forgive" by placing people into God's hands! We forgive them, but hope God will judge them!

A SUBTLE BUT IMPORTANT DISTINCTION EXISTS BETWEEN OUR FORGIVING OF OTHERS AND FURTHERMORE WANTING GOD TO FORGIVE THEM AS WELL.

When Jesus said, "Father forgive them," he was teaching us that beyond our own forgiveness of others, we are to wish, hope and even pray for God's blessing upon them. Reaching the point of being able to bless our enemies shows not only that we have forgiven from the heart, but also that we truly understand the heart of Our Good Heavenly Father. Jesus taught, "You have heard that it was said, 'Love your neighbor and hate your enemy.' But I tell you, love your enemies and pray for those who persecute you, that you may be children of your Father in heaven."[9]

FINDING THE FATHER'S HEALING

After my experience at that altar, my eyes were opened to a whole new realm of spirituality that I had never known before. Prior to this experience, I had ascribed to what Peter Scazzero describes as "spirituality divorced from emotional health—one that allows deep, underlying layers of our lives to remain untouched by God."[10] I began to realize that God's heart is to heal us internally in this life, not just to save us for the next.

BEYOND FORGIVING OUR SINS, THE FATHER HAS SENT JESUS TO PROVIDE HIS HEALING FOR EVERY SIN EVER COMMITTED AGAINST US.

Before this encounter, if asked the question, "Do you want God to forgive all your sins?" my response would have been an unequivocal,

---

9   Matthew 5:43-45a

10 Scazzero, Peter. Emotionally Healthy Spirituality: Unleash a Revolution in Your Life In Christ (p. 20). Thomas Nelson. Kindle Edition.

"Yes!". If asked "Do you want God to heal all your wounds?" I would have probably looked at you with a blank stare. After this experience, I realized that beyond forgiving our sins, the Father has sent Jesus to provide his healing for every sin ever committed against us.

Receiving forgiveness for our sins comes when we humbly admit our need of pardon and the Father based on the sacrificial death of Jesus which takes away the penalty of the sins we have committed. God's Word promises, "If we confess our sins, he is faithful and just and will forgive us our sins and purify us from all unrighteousness."[11] The first form of healing we receive from the Father comes when we admit our faults and allow him to remove the guilt and shame associated with our sins.

> *IT IS ON THE BASIS OF THE FORGIVENESS WE FIRST RECEIVED THAT WE ARE EMPOWERED TO FORGIVE OTHERS.*

The second wave of healing comes when we *extend* the same forgiveness we ourselves received to all those who have hurt or betrayed us. It is on the basis of the forgiveness we first received that we are empowered to forgive others. As Paul writes, "Be kind and compassionate to one another, forgiving each other, *just as* in Christ God forgave you."[12]

> *AS WE FORGIVE OTHERS, WE OPEN OURSELVES UP TO THE HEALING VIRTUE AND MERCY OF GOD THE FATHER.*

Healing begins when we agree with the words of Jesus spoken to the Father from the cross and make them our own, "Father, I forgive them". As we forgive others, we open ourselves up to the healing virtue and mercy of God the Father. It is in forgiving others that we are healed. In his book, *Total Forgiveness*, R.T. Kendall masterfully describes the dichotomy between forgiving others and the healing we receive in exchange. Kendall writes:

> *The paradox in total forgiveness is that it simultaneously involves selfishness and unselfishness. It is selfish- in that you do not want to hurt yourself by holding on to bitterness; And [sic] it is unselfish in that you commit yourself to the well-being*

11 1 John 1:9
12 Ephesians 4:32, italics added

of your enemy! You could almost say that total forgiveness is both extreme selfishness and extreme unselfishness. You are looking out for your own interests when you totally forgive, but you are also totally setting your offender free.[13]

→ *this is me*

THEY DON'T KNOW WHAT THEY DO

Receiving forgiveness sounds wonderful. Finding healing sounds refreshing. Extending forgiveness to those who have hurt us, well, that is going to take some more serious consideration. As much as we want to forgive others for the benefit of finding healing, we may have a hard time letting them off the hook for the ways they have transgressed us. We can read beyond Jesus' initial three words, "Father, forgive them" and become stuck when we hear him also say, "for they do not know what they are doing."

Corrie ten Boom recounts the story of meeting one of the concentration camp guards in a former prison where she and her sister Betsie were once held captive. After completing a talk on God's complete forgiveness of our sins at a church in Munich, Germany, the man came up front extending his hand and asking for her forgiveness. She recounts her sentiments in the moment.

And I, who had spoken so glibly of forgiveness, fumbled in my pocketbook rather than take that hand...Betsie had died in that place—could he erase her slow terrible death simply for the asking? It could not have been many seconds that he stood there, hand held out, but to me it seemed hours as I wrestled with the most difficult thing I had ever had to do.[14]

When we consider the people who have offended and hurt us, oftentimes they seemed to very much know what they were doing. Their unkind words and insults along with their physical, verbal or mental abuse were in our own estimation quite deliberate and intentional. "They certainly *did* know what they were doing!" we protest.

---

13 Kendell, R.T. (2002) *Total Forgiveness*. Charisma House. p.163.
14 Guideposts Classics: Corrie ten Boom on Forgiveness, https://www.guideposts.org/betterliving/positive-living/guideposts-classics-corrie-ten-boom-on-forgiveness, accessed February 20, 2017.

And maybe we're right. Maybe our offenders wanted to do us harm. Maybe they truly did intend to hurt us. Maybe the rejection and pain they dished out to us was not random or by chance, but very much premeditated and spiteful in nature. If that's the case, why would we ever want to let them off the hook with the words, "Father, forgive them."?

Let's be honest, forgiving others as God has forgiven us may be biblical, but it does not mean it will be easy especially when we start to ask ourselves why they did what they did. We will never be able to peer into the hearts of others to understand not only their motives, but also discern their entire psychological, spiritual, cultural and emotional frame of reference. We cannot really figure out why people do the wrongs they do. We have a hard-enough time figuring out why we do the wrong things that we ourselves do! As the Apostle Paul confessed, "I do not understand what I do. For what I want to do I do not do, but what I hate I do."[15]

OUR JOB IS NOT TO UNDERSTAND WHY OUR OFFENDERS MADE THE CHOICES THEY MADE, BUT TO LET GOD BE THE ULTIMATE JUDGE AND TURN OVER THE KEYS OF OUR RESENTMENT, BITTERNESS AND UNFORGIVENESS TO HIM.

Our job is not to understand why our offenders made the choices they made, but to let God be the ultimate judge and turn over the keys of our resentment, bitterness and unforgiveness to him. We hand him the keys of our heart and say, "Father, I forgive them." As Kendall says, "Judging people is elbowing in on God's exclusive territory."[16] We must make the choice to forgive, even when our feelings do not measure up. As Corrie ten Boom looked at the hand extended to her, she knew the right thing to do was to forgive, even if her feelings did not match.

And still I stood there with the coldness clutching my heart. But forgiveness is not an emotion—I knew that too. Forgiveness is an act of the will, and the will can function regardless of the

---

15 Romans 7:15

16 Kendell, R.T. (2002) *Total Forgiveness*. Charisma House. p.104.

temperature of the heart. "Jesus, help me!" I prayed silently. "I can lift my hand. I can do that much. You supply the feeling."[17]

When we choose to forgive, do we justify the hurts we have received? By no means. Is it to walk around like a human punching bag just waiting for the next person to dole out another round of hurtful blows? Not at all. Is it to set ourselves up for further hurt and pain by the people who have betrayed our trust? That's not the goal.

Instead, we are to look at the cross and recognize that when Jesus prayed, "Father, forgive them", he was including you and me. We were the ones who Jesus forgave, not just the people who crucified him and not just the people who have hurt us along the way. Jesus died so we could be forgiven and set free, in order for us to then offer the same pardon to those who have wronged us.[18]

By reciprocating the same gift of forgiveness to others that God in Christ gave to us, we open our hearts to the healing power of the Father. As we turn over the keys of judgment to the Father, we unlock the healing power of God to flow freely in our lives. Corrie ten Boom recounts of how the story ends.

And so woodenly, mechanically, I thrust my hand into the one stretched out to me. And as I did, an incredible thing took place. The current started in my shoulder, raced down my arm, sprang into our joined hands. And then this healing warmth seemed to flood my whole being, bringing tears to my eyes. "I forgive you, brother!" I cried. "With all my heart!" For a long moment we grasped each other's hands, the former guard and the former prisoner. I had never known God's love so intensely as I did then.[19]

I encourage you to take time alone, in the presence of Our Good Father, and welcome him to bring healing and wholeness into your own heart and life based on the death of his son Jesus. Emotions are not a requirement as much as the choice to give forgiveness and

---

17 Guideposts Classics: Corrie ten Boom on Forgiveness, https://www.guideposts. org/better-living/positiveliving/guideposts-classics-corrie-ten-boom-on-forgiveness, accessed February 20, 2017.

18 See also "The Parable of the Unmerciful Servant", Matthew 18:21-35.

19 Guideposts Classics: Corrie ten Boom on Forgiveness, https://www.guideposts. org/better-living/positiveliving/guideposts-classics-corrie-ten-boom-on-forgiveness, accessed February 20, 2017.

receive healing. As you silence your heart before God our Father, ask this one important question, "Who do I need to forgive?" And as the names, events and memories begin to come knocking on the door of your heart and mind, choose to respond with these words, "Father, I forgive them."

Points to Remember:

- Jesus came not only to forgive our sins, but to bring healing to the pain we experience through the sins of others.
- Our Good Father sent Jesus as his delegate to release his healing into our brokenness.
- It is on the basis of the forgiveness we first received that we are empowered to forgive others.
- As we forgive others, we open ourselves up to the healing virtue and mercy of God the Father.

Prayer:

"Father, I choose to forgive every person who has ever wounded me. Come, heal me."

Meditation:

Father, forgive them.

Group Discussion:

- How do you feel about the statement, "We all need healing"?
- If someone took a cross-section of your tree of life, how would it look on the inside?
- Who is a person in your life, or in human history, that models a lifestyle of genuine forgiveness towards others? What do you appreciate or respect about this person?

Dig Deeper:

Read through the following verses to learn more about the healing power of the Father.

- Luke 23:34: Jesus said, "Father, forgive them, for they do not know what they are doing."
- Isaiah 53:3-5: He was despised and rejected by mankind, a man of suffering, and familiar with pain. Like one from whom people hide their faces he was despised, and we held him in low esteem. Surely he took up our pain and bore our suffering, yet we considered him punished by God, stricken by him, and afflicted. But he was pierced for our transgressions, he was crushed for our iniquities; the punishment that brought us peace was on him, and by his wounds we are healed.
- 1 John 1:9: If we confess our sins, he is faithful and just and will forgive us our sins and purify us from all unrighteousness.
- Ephesians 4:32: Be kind and compassionate to one another, forgiving each other, just as in Christ God forgave you.

CHAPTER SEVEN

A FATHER WHO GUIDES US

*"For each one of us, there is only one thing necessary:
to fulfill our own destiny, according to God's will, to be what
God wants us to be."*

— THOMAS MERTON

I came to know Christ personally at the age of twenty-two. Prior to my conversion, I had received my fair share of religious education, but I never truly knew God for myself. Coming to know God, not just about God, made a profound difference in my life and perspective. Spirituality was no longer a matter of going to church or through the religious motions. Instead it became a metamorphosis of my life, first internally then externally.

One of the biggest changes I recognized in myself after my salvation experience was the desire to know God's will. Prior to having God living within me, my interests were all centered around what I wanted in life. I would ask myself: "Where do **I** want to go to school? What type of work do **I** want to do? How do **I** want to use **my** free time?" "How do **I** want to spend **my** money?" I was the center of my life, the captain of my own ship, the piñata of my own party.

DESIRING TO DO GOD'S WILL

Once God came into the picture, I began to ask a new question: "What is God's will for my life?" This question had never before so much as scratched the surface of my mind. Now it was blossoming as beautifully as a spring flower. My focus had changed from being me-centered to being God-centered. I wanted to learn what God's desires were instead of just fixating on what I wanted to get out of life.

The desire to do God's will has been a longing of God's people throughout time. A thousand years before the birth of Christ, King David phrased it this way in Psalm 40:8: "I delight to do your will, O my God; your law is within my heart."[1]

> **THE DESIRE TO DO GOD'S WILL IS A SUPERNATURAL GIFT FROM THE FATHER.**

As children of God, the desire to do what is pleasing to the Father and to avoid living outside of his will has been imparted to us. The desire to do God's will is a supernatural gift from the Father.

Our desire to do God's will increases proportionately with our understanding and trust in the goodness of Father God. When we grasp the goodness of the Father, we pray in earnest and without reservation "your kingdom come, your will be done" in my life, my family, our church, community, city and nation.

Yet at times desiring to do God's will seems easier than discerning his will. Knowing what God wants from us can feel a bit mysterious and nebulous, especially when the choice we need to make is between two seemingly good options.

> **THE DESIRE TO DO GOD'S WILL INCREASES PROPORTIONATELY WITH OUR UNDERSTANDING AND TRUST IN THE GOODNESS OF FATHER GOD.**

Thankfully, Jesus gives us in his well-known Sermon on the Mount, a simple, yet profound solution to finding the Father's will for our lives. This solution can be summarized in three words: ask, seek, and knock.

> Ask and it will be given to you; seek and you will find; knock and the door will be opened to you. For everyone who asks receives; the one who seeks finds; and to the one who knocks, the door will be opened. Which of you, if your son asks for bread, will give him a stone? Or if he asks for a fish, will give him a snake? If you, then, though you are evil, know how to give good gifts to your children, how much more will your Father in heaven give good gifts to those who ask him![2]

---

1   Psalm 40:8, ESV
2   Matthew 7:7-11

GUARANTEES

I like guarantees. "Money back guarantee" are three words that can provide a small sense of security in a vastly uncertain world. Anyone who is willing to put their money where their proverbial mouth is must have confidence in their product or service. Just today, in fact, I spoke with a representative of a company that promises a full money-back guarantee if their product doesn't boost a client's annual sales by five percent. That's a pretty impressive guarantee!

Jesus gives us three even more extraordinary guarantees when it comes to our search for the Father's will in our lives:

- Ask and it **will** be given to you.
- Seek and you **will** find.
- Knock and the door **will** be opened to you.

Jesus didn't say "could be given" or "might find" or "likely to open". He said "will". I would venture to say that sounds like a guarantee. How often do we take Jesus at his word and believe that if we truly do ask, we will be given? That if we truly do seek, we will find. And if we knock persistently, the door will eventually open.

Jesus offers these guarantees to all people: "For **everyone** who asks receives; the one who seeks finds; and to the one who knocks, the door will be opened." The word "everyone" shows no discrimination. It is the same word translated as "whosoever" in John 3:16: "For God so loved the world, that he gave his only begotten Son, that **whosoever** believes in him should not perish, but have everlasting life." Unless you find a way to not be part of everyone, which would be difficult, these guarantees are offered to you.

HINDRANCES

Truth be told, as much as I like guarantees, I don't always act upon them. I don't really have a good excuse as to why I avoid such offers. At times I forget the guarantees that have been offered to me. Other times, I misplace the offer or get too busy to bother with the guaranteed promise. Maybe you are different than me and you routinely take companies or people up on their guarantees or promises. For whatever reason, I too often just settle for the assured feelings of a guarantee instead of acting upon the credibility of the offer.

It is not uncommon for us to avoid acting on God's promises for our lives in the same way I neglect acting on a guarantee. In fact, I see three main hindrances—apart from forgetfulness—that keep us from acting on the guarantees Jesus offers and wholeheartedly asking, seeking, and knocking on God's door.

- The first hindrance is one of intellect.
- The second hindrance is one of theology.
- The third hindrance is one of experience.

Let's first tackle the **intellectual** hindrance. This particular obstacle takes a promise like "ask and it will be given to you", but rather than receiving it gladly as a child receives a delicious ice cream cone, we instead examine it like a scientist looking into a glass beaker filled with some unknown substance. We hold it up, measure it, and shake it, analyzing the promise to figure out whether or not it might be valid before making any attempt to try it for ourselves. It would be like that child with the ice cream cone just watching it melt and musing aloud, "I wonder if this was made from whole milk or 2%." Father's promises are more like ice cream than beakers. He wants us to enjoy them with childlike glee, not examine them to death.

The second hindrance to receiving these great promises by faith is **theological**. In this obstacle, we believe that Father's will just happens no matter what, so our prayers really have no effect. We say or at least think thoughts like: "If it's God's will, he'll just make it happen anyway, so what's the point of praying?" Before we ever ask, we start to eliminate possibilities of how God can answer our prayers by our false theological trappings.

> JACOB WAS SO OBSTINATE FOR THE GOODNESS OF GOD THAT HE WOULD NOT SETTLE FOR ANYTHING LESS THAN GOD'S BLESSING ON HIS LIFE.

When a child comes to a benevolent parent to ask for a particular blessing, they confidently and boldly expect something good in return. Even if the parent says "no", children may have a back-up plan or a follow-up argument to try to change their parent's mind. We, in contrast, too often avoid persistence in prayer, settling for what we assume to be Our Father's will instead of persevering like the biblical patriarch Jacob who, after wrestling with God in human form all night, told God:

"I will not let you go unless you bless me."[3] Jacob was so obstinate for the goodness of God that he would not settle for anything less than God's blessing on his life.

The third hindrance to our banking on God's promises in true faith is that of our own past experiences. Disappointing experiences in particular tend to wear down the tires of our faith in God. We may offer as rationale: "I prayed for my wife to be healed, and she died." Or "The last time I asked God for a job I didn't get it." Instead of focusing on God's promise at hand, we turn our attention to previous losses, disappointment, or unanswered prayer. It is like a football team entering into a new game and saying, "Well, we lost the last three games, so why even try this time?" True faith does not quit because of past perceived failures. True faith looks at every challenge like a new game. True faith proclaims: We can win this battle because the Lord is on our side! Past disappointments do not predict future outcomes.

PAST DISAPPOINTMENTS DO NOT PREDICT FUTURE OUTCOMES.

ASK

Jesus said, "Ask and it will be given to you". The word "ask" in this passage comes from a Greek word, *aiteo*.[4] I appreciate how the Spirit-Filled Life Bible commentary describes this word:

> This word usually describes a suppliant making request of someone in higher position, such as an individual asking something from God, a subject from a king, a child from a parent or a beggar from a person of substance. The word denotes insistent asking without qualms, not 'commanding God', but solidly presenting a requisition whose items He longs to distribute.[5]

Three things must hold true in order for a person to ask something from another person or God.

- First, recognition of one's own needs or sense of dependency.
- Second, the humility to ask another person for help. Pride keeps

---

3 Genesis 32:26

4 Strong's Greek Dictionary #154

5 Spirit-Filled Life Bible, Word Wealth, Matthew 7:7, page 1416.

us from admitting our own need or being willing to receive the assistance of another.

• Third, a level of faith and confidence that the person to whom our request is made is both willing and able to meet our expressed need.

If we are to come to God and ask for our needs to be met, we must believe that he is interested and able to meet our demands for help. As the author of the New Testament book of Hebrews writes in what is commonly termed the Hall of Faith chapter:

And without faith it is impossible to please God, because anyone who comes to him must believe that he exists and that he rewards those who earnestly seek him.[6]

The good news is that Father God is more than willing and more than able to take our requests and answer our petitions. Seeking the Father's will in our lives begins by asking him for his assistance, grace,

FINDING GOD'S WILL ALWAYS STARTS WITH ASKING.

wisdom, favor and every other good gift or virtue we can think of or imagine. Finding God's will always starts with asking.

SEEK

The words "seek" and "knock" are often taught as additional emphases on prayer. Asking is often taught to be the first level of prayer. Seeking is therefore seen as a more intense level. Knocking is like pounding-on-the-door of prayer: "God, are you there? Then please come open the door!"

From my experience in walking with the Father, I have learned that prayer is the first step in discovering the Father's will. But it is only one portion of the equation. I have found that God longs for us to pray, but he doesn't want us to stop there. Prayer is a conversation that God wants us to initiate. But in our relationship with the Father, we must go beyond asking in prayer to seeking and knocking.

If asking happens with our mouths, where does seeking take place? That's an easy one! It starts with our eyes. Seeking God's will means we begin to look around, search, and research for answers to our questions. This is the second phase of discovering the Father's will

6   Hebrews 11:6

for our lives. We begin the seeking stage by prayerfully reading God's Word, the Bible, and asking God to reveal his truth and will for our lives through the Holy Spirit.

Seeking begins with prayerful Bible study, but it does not end there. Seeking can take place through various forms of research and due diligence. In the information age we live in, we can easily look to our computers or phones to research and find out answers to many of life's questions. Searching a matter out may also include seeking wise counsel from people we know, trust, and who have a good track record of making wise choices or expertise in the subject matter at hand. To seek is to have our spiritual eyes open to discern and know all the facts as well as any ways in which God is leading us.

When we seek answers to our questions in a spirit of faith, we do so recognizing that we may not obtain all the answers, but we can gain greater knowledge and wisdom in order to make the best choices. As the biblical King Solomon stated wisely: "It is the glory of God to conceal a matter; to search out a matter is the glory of kings."[7]

I have a tendency to lose things. I'm telling you, I lose things all the time. In fact, if there were a title of "Professional Loser", I think I would qualify. The top three things I lose are my car keys, my wallet and my sunglasses. I think these three possessions are in cahoots taking turns hiding from me for the fun of it.

AS WE SEEK, IT DOES NOT MEAN WE STOP PRAYING. WE CAN BE PRAYING EVEN IN THE PROCESS OF OUR SEEKING.

Now when I lose something, the first thing I typically do is pray to God. "Lord, please help me to find my wallet." I tell you the angels in heaven must be tired of hearing that prayer request. "Doesn't this Loser have something more spiritual to pray for than finding his lost keys?" The first thing I do after I pray is to start searching around the house. Inevitably, God has a way of leading me to the items I have lost. I guess that makes him a "Professional Finder".

---

7   Proverbs 25:2

How absurd would it be, if I lost one of these items and prayed for it, but stayed on my knees with my eyes closed never bothering to get up and look for it? Wouldn't it be foolish to ask for my lost keys, but not seek them out as well? In the same way, asking in prayer but never seeking the answer is somewhat foolish. Don't you agree?

Let's say you are trying to discern whether it is Father's will to move to a different city. The "seeking" aspect of this journey may involve matters such as looking into costs of living, job opportunities, and schools for your kids. As we seek, it does not mean we stop praying. We can be praying even in the process of our seeking. "God, where are those keys?"

The Father has given us eyes and minds to search matters out, and he wants us to use them. It is his guaranteed promise that if we seek, we will find the answers we are looking for. Or at a minimum, answers sufficient enough for us to move forward in faith.

So what types of things do we seek after in life? Here are just a few that come from my own experience:

- We seek answers to our questions.
- We seek understanding.
- We seek for people to be found.
- We seek for meaning, significance, purpose.
- We seek for keys, wallets and sunglasses. (At least I do.)
- We seek counsel, advice.
- We seek clarity, direction, guidance.
- We seek God's kingdom purposes.

Our search for God's will starts with **asking** God, then moves to **seeking** God's will in the matter. But we need to take care not to get bogged down in the details or fall into "analysis paralysis" mode. Seeking is a good second step, but if we only seek answers and never respond in faith, we will fall short of God's will 100% of the time! We must follow seeking with **knocking**. Jesus promises: "to the one who knocks, the door will be opened."

IF WE ONLY SEEK ANSWERS AND NEVER RESPOND IN FAITH, WE WILL FALL SHORT OF GOD'S WILL 100% OF THE TIME!

KNOCK

If asking involves our mouths and seeking involves our eyes, then knocking involves our hands. Knocking means we take action based on the things we discover in prayer and research. We must move forward in faith, trusting God to open the door for us to walk through into God's intended destiny for our lives. The Bible provides many examples of doors being knocked on by people for a variety of purposes. One of my favorites is the story of Nehemiah.

> *KNOCKING MEANS WE TAKE ACTION BASED ON THE THINGS WE DISCOVER IN PRAYER AND RESEARCH.*

Nehemiah sought after God in prayer and fasting when he heard that the walls of Jerusalem were broken down and the gates burnt by fire. He prayed to God and took God at his word, asking God to show his power in redeeming his people. But Nehemiah did not stop with just prayer. He next sought after the assistance he needed from King Artaxerxes to be given a long-term leave of absence to rebuild the wall. Scripture tells us that "in the LORD's hand, the king's heart is a stream of water that he channels toward all who please him."[8] God moved upon King Artaxerxes' heart and opened the door wide for Nehemiah to walk through.

It was a bold move on Nehemiah's part to ask the King for such favor. It is this type of bold faith, prayer and action that pleases God our Father. As a prelude to the same passage on asking, seeking and knocking, the author Luke includes a story Jesus told about the importance of bold persistence.

> Then Jesus said to them, *"Suppose you have a friend, and you go to him at midnight and say, 'Friend, lend me three loaves of bread; a friend of mine on a journey has come to me, and I have no food to offer him.' And suppose the one inside answers, 'Don't bother me. The door is already locked, and my children and I are in bed. I can't get up and give you anything.' I tell you, even though he will not get up and give you the bread because of friendship, yet because of your shameless audacity he will surely get up and give you as much as you need.*[9]

8   Proverbs 21:1
9   Luke 11:5-8, italics added

If bold persistence can persuade a king and move upon a man in the middle of the night, how much more will Our Good Father honor the persistent cry of his children? Jesus tells a similar story of a judge who "neither feared God nor cared what people thought" yet was persuaded by the persistence of a widow's request.[10] Jesus ends his story with two rhetorical questions, "And will not God bring about justice for his chosen ones, who cry out to him day and night? Will he keep putting them off?"[11] Our Father's heart is wide open to our cries and prayers!

> *OUR FATHER'S HEART IS WIDE OPEN TO OUR CRIES AND PRAYERS!*

OPEN HEARTS

Speaking of open hearts and answered prayers, my writing of this chapter marks eight months since I had heart surgery. At only thirty-eight years of age, I needed to go under the knife to take care of a congenital heart problem that had gotten progressively worse over time. My cardiologist had suggested that, since I was in good overall health and did not have any symptoms, it would be a wise time to move forward with the surgery.

Walking through the process of heart surgery is a great example within my own life experience of discovering and doing the Father's will by asking, seeking and knocking. As I've mentioned previously, the Father's will is first found through asking him, i.e. through prayer. It is then found through seeking out answers. Lastly, it is acted upon by faith as we knock on the doors God is opening in our lives.

My asking involved not only my own prayers, but the prayers of my family members and my church community. I was asking for them to pray for God's leading and guidance, but also for a miracle. I believe in God's healing power and had received divine healing previously, so I was not only asking God for wisdom and guidance, but for his supernatural intervention to fix my heart issue.

After my cardiologist's initial diagnosis and recommendation, I proceeded to have further testing as well as second, third, and fourth

---

10 Luke 18:1-6
11 Luke 18:7

opinions. The tests and appointments with other cardiologists and cardiac surgeons were all part of my seeking process. All the tests and the recommendations by the doctors seemed to point in the same conclusion, which was that surgery was inevitable and the sooner I had it, the better.

Once I made the determination to get the surgery done, I started my search for the right surgeon. I created a spreadsheet with information on all the available doctors, whether or not they performed the surgery in a minimally invasive fashion (which was my personal preference), and whether or not they were covered by my health insurance. After this extensive search, my decision came down to one of two surgeons. I chose the surgeon with the greatest experience and highest reputation in the field.

After taking into consideration all the prayers, prods, and personal preferences, it was now time to act. I had to move forward in faith to get the surgery. It was a considerable step of faith for me to knock on the door and literally have my body opened up in surgery. After all, I was asymptomatic (experienced no symptoms of my condition), but had been told the surgery was inevitable. Who ever heard of preventative heart surgery? I am glad to say that the surgery was a complete success and that I am 100% back to normal.

OPEN EYES

The Father not only opens hearts and doors, he opens eyes. The king of Syria had planned an attack against Israel. Fortunately for Israel's sake, Elisha had prophetic insight into the Syrian king's plan and was able to notify and forewarn the king of Israel. When the king of Syria learned of Elisha's spiritual espionage, he found out where Elisha was staying, a city named Dothan.

One morning soon after, Elisha's servant woke up, walked out of the front door, and saw that the entire city was surrounded by horses, chariots and a great army belonging to the king of Syria. Talk about a serious wake-up call! This young man started to freak out, and with good reason. He went to Elisha to report the news, probably expecting Elisha to be equally petrified. But to the servant's surprise, God's prophet was as cool as a cucumber (just how cool is a cucumber, anyway?).

"Don't be afraid," the prophet told his servant. "Those who are with us are more than those who are with them." Then Elisha prayed: "Open his eyes, LORD, so that he may see." God opened the servant's eyes. When he looked out to where he'd seen the Syrian king's army, the servant could now see that the hills all around the city were filled with horses and chariots of fire from an angelic host protecting Elisha.[12]

Could it be that you are viewing your circumstances through the wrong lens? Maybe it's time for you to ask the Father to open your eyes so you can see your trial, tribulation, hardship, or even your opportunity with his perspective in mind.

Or maybe you need to pray for God to open the heart of an unbelieving spouse, relative, neighbor, or friend so they can see the glory of God's salvation found in Christ. We know from Scripture that "the god of this age has blinded the minds of unbelievers, so that they cannot see the light of the gospel that displays the glory of Christ, who is the image of God."[13] Thank God that we serve a Father who knows how to open eyes and hearts.

PARTNERING WITH FATHER

As a Good Father, God wants to guide his children in making wise choices for our lives. A father of young children tends to give directives about the right and wrong things a son or daughter is to do. As children, we learn what to touch and what not to touch, what to say and what not to say. The values, principles, boundaries and the dos and don'ts of life are instilled in us by our parents and elders to guide our life. As the child matures, she starts to gain greater responsibility in making her own life choices and the role of the parent changes into one of guide, mentor or coach.

> *PRAYER IS THE ESSENTIAL STARTING BLOCK, BUT PRAYER ALONE WILL NOT GET US PAST THE FINISH LINE.*

Similarly, as we mature in our relationship with God, seeking his will becomes a partnership between us and the Father that starts in prayer. We come to God to ask him *for* things and also to talk with him *about* our life journey and decisions asking for wisdom and guidance to make the best choices.

12 2 Kings 6:18,19
13 2 Corinthians 4:4

The author of the New Testament epistle of James, believed by a majority of biblical scholars to be the brother of Jesus, wrote to the Church: "If any of you lacks wisdom, you should ask God, who gives generously to all without finding fault, and it will be given to you."[14] He went on to add, "You do not have because you do not ask God."[15]

Starting any journey in prayer helps to keep the communication lines open with heaven, not only for God to hear us, but for us to hear from the Father. We come to God asking for him to provide for us and also for him to guide us in our journey. If we avoid prayer, we are setting ourselves up for increased and unnecessary struggle, heartache, burdens, trials, and difficulties.

But if we make the mistake of reducing God's will down to prayer and prayer only, we will not get very far in the journey either. Prayer is the essential starting block, but prayer alone will not get us past the finish line. Prayer is woven throughout our journey of seeking Our Good Father's will, but it is not the summation of the trip. We must pray, and then we must seek.

Seeking is essential because with increased knowledge we have greater awareness of our surroundings, opportunities, potentials risks, as well as rewards. If you buy a car without doing the proper research and due diligence about the particular make and model, you may end up finding yourself becoming a better friend with your mechanic than you'd like. Seeking is the honorable responsibility of every steward of God's kingdom because God wants us to learn how to go after the truth in all areas of life. He wants us to become mature children who learn and discern how to make wise decisions.

IF WE SEEK AND AVOID ACTION, OUR TANKS GET FILLED UP WITH GREATER KNOWLEDGE, BUT OUR LIVES STAY IN NEUTRAL. WE MUST ACT UPON WHAT WE LEARN.

Seeking the answers is an important step to finding God's will, but it is not the final step. If we seek and avoid action, our tanks get filled up with greater knowledge, but our lives stay in neutral. We must act upon what we learn. We need to knock on the doors that God opens and move forward in good faith through them. Having knowledge with

14 James 1:5
15 James 4:2c

no action is like being a politician who gives great speeches, but never legislates. All talk, but no action leads to great dissatisfaction.

It is important to note that at times, after praying and seeking, we may come to the conclusion that God wants us to wait or not to take the next step. He may be warning us to not proceed forward or cautioning us to slow down and wait upon his timing. Knocking does not mean we must proceed forward with a particular decision. It does mean we must choose to be responsible for our decision and not allow indecision to become our choice. In these three steps we have just discussed, we learn how the Father works alongside his children:

- We ask. Father gives.
- We seek. Father guides.
- We knock. Father empowers.

ARE YOU BETTER THAN GOD?

When teaching the Sermon on the Mount, Jesus followed up his advice of asking, seeking, and knocking by asking his audience two questions: "Which of you, if your son asks for bread, will give him a stone? Or if he asks for a fish, will give him a snake?"[16] Jesus, the master of rhetorical questions, did not expect a response. But his point is clear. A child who asks a good parent for something they want will not receive something bad in return.

HOW IS IT THAT WE CAN HAVE SUCH CONFIDENCE IN OUR OWN GOODNESS AND YET AT TIMES LACK A SIMILAR TRUST AND FAITH IN FATHER GOD'S GOODNESS?

It's time for a true confession. **Sometimes I think I am better than God!** Let me explain. As a father, I know it is in my heart to give my children only the best in life. Even when I say "no", it is because I want what's best for my kids in every way possible.

That's not to say I don't make mistakes and that I have not and will not err in my judgment, attitude, actions, or inaction. I'm just saying that my heart's desire and intention is for my children's best, both now and in their future. How is it that I can have such confidence in my own good nature and yet at times lack a similar trust and faith in Father God's goodness? If I doubt God's goodness, but trust my own as a parent, I

---

16 Matthew 7:9

make myself out to be better than God. That is a scary proposition!

Jesus wants us to know that we can have absolute confidence that Father God is working diligently on our behalf and that he wants to hear the requests of our heart. He put it this way:

> *If you, then, though you are evil, know how to give good gifts to your children, how much more will your Father in heaven give good gifts to those who ask him!*[17]

If a flawed individual like me can have the mind and heart to want to bless my children, how much more does a perfect heavenly Father desire to bless us, his kids, with every good thing? Consider these questions:

- Do you trust the Father enough to ask him for the things that are on your heart?
- Do you believe the Father to be good at heart and to never give you something harmful, evil, or bad?
- If you knew with complete certainty that God would never give you anything bad, no matter what you asked for, how would it change the way you pray?

The next time you seek the Father's will for your life, keep Jesus in mind. God's gift of Jesus to the world is the one sign we need to know the Father is good and that his will for our lives is ultimately good. As the apostle Paul summed it up: "He who did not spare his own Son, but gave him up for us all - how will he not also, along with him, graciously give us all things?"[18] Paul again writes concerning the will of the Father and describes it as "good, pleasing and perfect."[19] Therefore, as we pray for, seek after, and take action to do God's will on the earth, let's proceed forward with confidence and trust that no matter how things may appear on the outside, Father God is working on our side and his plans for our lives are truly good.

---

17 Matthew 7:11
18 Romans 8:32
19 Romans 12:2

Points to Remember:

- Jesus guarantees that if we ask, seek and knock, Father will respond to us.
- Finding God's will starts with asking.
- Seeking is about searching for the right answers and seeing God's leading in a matter.
- Knocking requires us to take action and not just accumulate knowledge.

Prayer:

"Good Father, I ask you for good things. I will seek your answers and I will respond in faith."

Meditation:

Father is guiding my life.

Group Discussion:

- In which area of your life would you like to have greater clarity about God's will?
- If you had to make a major decision, who are some of the people you would talk to about it?
- What is the greatest step of faith you feel you have taken so far in your life?

Dig Deeper:

Read through the following verses to study more about God's guidance and will.

- Matthew 7:7-11: Ask and it will be given to you; seek and you will find; knock and the door will be opened to you. For everyone who asks receives; the one who seeks finds; and to the one who knocks, the door will be opened. Which of you, if your son asks for bread, will give him a stone? Or if he asks for a fish, will give him a snake?

If you, then, though you are evil, know how to give good gifts to your children, how much more will your Father in heaven give good gifts to those who ask him!

- Hebrews 11:6: And without faith it is impossible to please God, because anyone who comes to him must believe that he exists and that he rewards those who earnestly seek him.
- Proverbs 25:2: It is the glory of God to conceal a matter; to search out a matter is the glory of kings.

CHAPTER EIGHT

Words to be Savored

"Do you wish to find out the really sublime?
Repeat the Lord's Prayer."

— NAPOLEON BONAPARTE

As mentioned previously, I grew up in the Maronite Catholic tradition of my Lebanese heritage. As a young boy, I would occasionally drift into the confessional to talk to the priest about my sins. My game plan going in was always to confess the same three sins: "I lied. I stole. I cheated." I figured those were safe enough transgressions to admit to the local priest in my small hometown without any serious repercussions.

Thankfully, the priest never dug for more information. Instead he would just dole out the prayers I was to pray as penance and the number of repetitions he (and presumably God) wanted me to say of those prayers. I would dutifully exit, find a pew, and get to praying as fast as I could. One of the most typically assigned prayers was the one Jesus gave to his disciples as an example of how to pray, now known commonly as the Lord's Prayer:

> *Our Father in heaven, hallowed be Your name. Your kingdom come. Your will be done on earth as it is in heaven. Give us this day our daily bread. And forgive us our debts, as we forgive our debtors. And do not lead us into temptation, but deliver us from the evil one. For Yours is the kingdom and the power and the glory forever. Amen.[1]*

Now, no one has ever recorded me, but I am confident that I can say the Lord's Prayer faster than anyone else on the planet. I had a lot

---

1   Matthew 6:9-13, NKJV

of practice. Now, not even the best auctioneer or fastest rapper could speak those words as quickly as I can.

The speed of my post-confessional prayer time makes me think of my dog Angel. Angel's diet is typically dry dog food. I'm sure if it were up to my kids, she'd be eating Filet Mignon every night, but for now we're sticking to the dry bagged stuff. Whenever we spoil little Ms. Angel with some chicken from the table, that girl inhales it like an Oreck vacuum cleaner. My guess is that she's afraid if she waits too long, we might take it away. She wolfs it down whole. In the same way, I used to pray through the Lord's Prayer as quick as I could to get it down, done with and move on to the next thing in my day.

> *JESUS WAS NOT JUST TEACHING HIS DISCIPLES A LESSON ON PRAYER. HE WAS TEACHING THEM ABOUT LIVING LIFE.*

The Lord's Prayer was not intended for quick consumption or rote repetition. It is a prayer that deserves to be chewed slowly, savored deeply, and digested fully. If we process this prayer at the right tempo, it has the potential to not only change the nature of our relationship with Father God, but our attitude, behavior, priorities, and lifestyle. When Jesus gave his disciples what we now call the Lord's Prayer as an example of how to pray, Jesus was not just teaching his disciples a lesson on prayer. He was teaching them about living life.

WHO IS PRAYING?

Research has shown that 55% of Americans pray on a daily basis.[2] That is a lot of prayer! If every one of those praying people said only one prayer a day, that would equate to 160 million prayers a day. Just to give that number some perspective, the president of the United States "only" gets 100,000 emails a week.[3] So God gets more requests in one day than all the emails combined for every U.S. president over the next thirty years!

---

2 Lipka, Michael. "5 facts about prayer". "Pew Research Center". May 4, 2017. http://www.pewresearch.org/fact-tank/2016/05/04/5-facts-about-prayer/, accessed June 2, 2017.

3 Smith, Stephen. "How many letters does the president receive daily?" December 30, 2009. http://www.ajc.com/news/news/local/q-how-many-letters-does-the-presidentreceive-dail/nQbMN/, accessed June 2, 2017.

But I have to wonder. How many of those prayers God receives are like the ones I prayed after confession? How many of them are rote and perfunctory, done out of a sense of obligation or habit? I believe the Father wants more out of our conversation with him than just repeated words. He wants more out of our lives than just lip service.

Looking back on the way I used to pray through the Lord's Prayer, I find it unfortunate that I was praying at such high speeds without giving the words I was speaking any real thought. Now that I have matured, not only in years, but in my relationship with God, I have taken the time to ponder the Lord's Prayer with greater appreciation.

In this chapter I have broken down this momentous prayer into smaller bite-sized portions. My hope is that you will enjoy this delicious spiritual meal that I am serving you and allow its truth to saturate your heart. As a suggestion, you may want to read this chapter in small bite-size chunks, like courses of a meal, instead of rushing through it all in one sitting.

"OUR FATHER ..."

The first words of the Lord's Prayer set the direction for our conversation with God. Jesus taught us to pray to "our" Father, not "my" Father. The Father that Jesus is presenting to us has a family. If you believe in Christ like I do, then I am your brother and the Christian down the block or seated next to you at church is your sister. We are a family, and families by definition consist of more than one person. So if you only pray on behalf of yourself, you have missed out on one essential element of prayer and also of life.

> THE FATHER DOES NOT DEFINE HIMSELF BY WHAT HE DOES OR HAS DONE, BUT INSTEAD ON THE RELATIONSHIP HE HAS WITH HIS CHILDREN.

We are to live in community, as members of a family, in connection with other people. Our prayer lives need to reflect our commitment to others. **Prayer is about community.**

The second word in this first phrase is just as revealing as the first. Jesus did not tell us to pray to "our Creator", although this title would be appropriate for God. The Father does not define himself by what he does or has done, but instead on the relationship he has with his children. He wants to be known as a Father.

I can relate. When I left the business world for fulltime church ministry, being called "Pastor" took some getting used to, especially when people who called me that were older than me. I told a guy the other week: "Just call me Pierre." Pastor seems too formal. Not to mention, I feel I should act a lot holier with a title like that! Contrarily, I can never get enough of my kids calling me "Dad" or "Daddy". Every time I hear that name, my heart swells up with great joy and satisfaction.

Jesus also did not instruct us to pray to "our Higher Power" because God is much more than just a force. God is a person. Too often we classify people based on their level of importance in their profession. We exalt professional athletes and actors and look with envy upon the world's wealthiest individuals. Yet God, who is the most amazing celebrity of all with the highest net worth, prefers to be referred to as Father. More than any other title, God desires the world to know that he is a family man. ***Prayer is about family.***

"... IN HEAVEN"

If you decided to write the president a letter to bump his emails up to 100,001 a week, you would need his email address. If you wanted to send me a postcard from your latest summer vacation, you would need my home address. Likewise, if you want to reach Father God in prayer, you must know where he resides. According to Jesus, our Father is in heaven. That is his mailing address.

Understanding that God is in heaven puts our prayers into perspective. King Solomon, the son of King David and Israel's most powerful king, put it this way:

> *Do not be quick with your mouth, do not be hasty in your heart to utter anything before God. God is in heaven and you are on earth, so let your words be few.*[4]

What did Solomon mean? Should we hold back the number of words we speak to God? Is there a quota? I don't think that was his point. It's the same advice you would give to anyone writing to the president. Even those of an opposing political view should have enough dignity to speak to the president with respect and honor and

---

4   Ecclesiastes 5:2

carefully weigh out their words. How much more reverence does God who is in heaven deserve from us? *Prayer is about reverence.*

STRIKING THE RIGHT BALANCE

In one sense, prayer to the Father is about family. It is about intimacy and closeness with Our Heavenly Father, who is full of love and compassion for his children. It is about climbing onto our Father's lap, looking into his eyes, and saying, "Daddy". It is about getting so close to God that you feel his presence residing not just all around you, but deeply within you. *Prayer is totally about relationship.*

But if you flip over the coin of prayer, you find that the other side reads "reverence". Prayer is also about recognizing who you are speaking to and the respect he deserves. Conversation with God, which is what we are doing when we pray, is not something we should approach flippantly.

In this dichotomy, there is also great harmony. Relationship without reverence would make God into a buddy, a vending machine, or a genie in a bottle. Reverence without relationship makes God a tyrant who must be appeased out of fear.

What does it look like to have a relationship with God that is both relational and reverential? One great depiction of such relationship and reverence comes from the presidency of John F. Kennedy. His son, JFK Jr. was the first child born to a sitting president. Jacqueline Kennedy, his wife, was opposed to pictures of her children being taken for political purposes. During a trip Jacqueline took out of the country, famed photojournalist Alan Stanley Tretick took a few iconic shots of JFK, Sr. and his three-year-old son in the Oval Office.[5]

RELATIONSHIP WITHOUT REVERENCE WOULD MAKE GOD INTO A BUDDY, A VENDING MACHINE OR A GENIE IN A BOTTLE. REVERENCE WITHOUT RELATIONSHIP MAKES GOD A TYRANT WHO MUST BE APPEASED OUT OF FEAR.

In these pictures, you see little John sitting under his dad's desk

---

5   Iconic Photos. "John F. Kennedy Jnr. under the Resolute Desk", https://iconicphotos.org/2010/09/03/john-f-kennedy-jnr-under-the-resolute-desk/, accessed June 2, 2017.

and even peeking through the front of it almost as if he were playing hide and seek. Imagine the president of the United States, a position of great power and authority revered by people all over the world, with a little boy crawling around under his desk. To me, this is a great picture of what reverence and relationship look like with Abba Father. We, his children, are welcomed into his presence at all times, but with respect and honor for his position and authority.

"... HALLOWED BE YOUR NAME."

This next part of the Lord's Prayer never made sense to me as a kid. I think my problem was that I misunderstood the word "hallowed" for "hollow". Somehow I figured God's name was empty on the inside like a chocolate Easter Bunny. I figured it had to be the letter "o" in the middle of the name God that made his name hollow. That was my best childhood guess, and since no one bothered to explain it to me, I figured it must not have mattered too much anyway.

In actuality, the word hallowed comes from a Greek word that means "to make holy".[6] In a ceremonial sense, it would mean to make someone or something holy. The word is also translated as "sanctify" in the New Testament and is used to describe the process God uses to make his people holy. For example, Jesus prayed to the Father concerning his followers saying, "Sanctify them by the truth; your word is truth."[7] In other words, Jesus was saying, "God, make your people holy through the truth of your Word."

It makes sense to hear the word used to describe the process by which a Holy God works to make unholy people more like himself. But what does it mean for people who are imperfect and flawed to "hallow", or make holy, God's name? How on earth can we make God's name holy?

In this context, the word actually means to honor as holy. Jesus is teaching us to pray with a worshipful heart, recognizing that God is indeed holy. He is pure, blameless, innocent of any sin, and completely different from you and me. In this light, we are to regard his name with the utmost respect and honor. The third of the Ten Commandments reads, "You shall not misuse the name of the Lord your God, for the

---

6   Strong's Greek Dictionary, #37

7   John 17:17

Lord will not hold anyone guiltless who misuses his name."[8] Father God wants us to honor and respect his name. His name was never meant to be used in replacement or conjunction with a curse word! *Prayer is about worship.*

"YOUR KINGDOM COME, YOUR WILL BE DONE."

There are two main desires of the Father that Jesus teaches us to ask for in prayer. The first is to seek the coming of God's kingdom. The kingdom of God represents the rule and reign of God. In this world, many people are out to build things for themselves. We may be looking to build successful businesses, beautiful homes, loving families, or just wonderful memories. We are a people who like to build. The instinct to build and make things great is a godly one, part of the DNA designed into us as those created in the image and likeness of the Ultimate Builder. To pray for God's kingdom to come here on earth means that we are seeking to invest our time, talent, and resources to build what's important to God, namely his eternal family.

Secondly, we are to ask for God's will, meaning God's desires and purposes, to be accomplished. Jesus is teaching us here to ask and trust for God's will to take precedence over our own will. This means that we want God's priorities and preferences over our own. At times, his priorities and ours align well. At other times, they may differ.

TO TRULY PRAY FROM THE HEART FOR GOD'S KINGDOM TO COME AND HIS WILL TO BE DONE REQUIRES TWO THINGS. FIRST, WE MUST BELIEVE THAT HE IS GOOD. SECONDLY, WE MUST TRUST HIM IMPLICITLY.

In a marriage, when a husband and wife disagree, it gives an opportunity for either compromise or conflict. Sometimes you get a little bit of both. To pray "your will be done" is saying to God: "Even when we see things differently, I want what you want, not what I want." To truly pray from the heart for God's kingdom to come and his will to be done requires two things. First, we must believe that God is good. Secondly, we must trust him implicitly. *Prayer is about surrender.*

---

8   Exodus 20:7

"... ON EARTH AS IT IS IN HEAVEN."

Jesus came *from* the kingdom of heaven. When Jesus tells us to pray for the kingdom of God to come to earth, he already has a picture in mind. He knows what it is like to live in the Father's perfect kingdom and to see God reign in all places. Listen to what he had to say to his disciples on several occasions about his original home:

> For *I have come down from heaven* not to do my will but to do the will of him who sent me.[9]

> You are from below; *I am from above.* You are of this world; I am not of this world.[10]

> My kingdom *is not of this world.*[11]

Jesus also came *for* the kingdom of heaven. His ultimate mission was to bring the kingdom of heaven to this earth. He explains this also to his disciples:

> I must proclaim the good news of the kingdom of God to the other cities also; for I was sent for this purpose.[12]

> The time is fulfilled, and the kingdom of God has come near; repent, and believe in the good news.[13]

> And this good news of the kingdom will be proclaimed throughout the world, as a testimony to all the nations.[14]

Every time I get away on a vacation, two things happen. First, I begin to see life a bit more clearly, and my view of what really matters in life becomes crystallized. Secondly, I begin to have new vision for my life. I start to think of ways in which my life, relationships, work, and home can all improve. It's amazing what can happen when we take a break from our work. Thank God for vacations!

JESUS CAME FROM THE KINGDOM OF HEAVEN. JESUS CAME FOR THE KINGDOM OF HEAVEN.

---

9   John 6:38
10 John 8:23
11 John 18:36
12 Luke 4:43
13 Mark 1:15
14 Matthew 24:14

Before time began, Jesus was living in paradise with the Father. Now that's a pretty good place to be if you ask me. No death, no tears, no sorrow, no stress, nothing but unending joy ... sign me up! Jesus left the glory of heaven to be born into a decrepit world where sickness, disease, poverty, sin, and a whole plethora of problems hold sway. Analogous to my earlier description of receiving clarity while on vacation, Jesus came to this earth with the clarity of mind to truly see this world and know that there is something so much better, sweeter, and brighter accessible to us.

Jesus wants us to pray for this earth, our world, our country, neighborhood, homes, family and relationships to become more like heaven. Now there's a thought. How might we pray differently if we knew that the end goal was to see earth become more like heaven? Would it inspire greater vision and faith in our prayers? In heaven, God is the focus of EVERYTHING. In heaven, God's peace reigns in EVERYONE'S heart. In heaven, EVERYWHERE we go, we see the beauty of God at work. Heaven is one amazing place and it is Jesus' desire for earth!

To pray for God's kingdom to come and his will to be done on this earth as it is in heaven is nothing shy of praying for the miraculous, transformational power of the good news to spread like wildfire on this earth. It would mean a dramatic change in people's attitudes and actions. Marriages would be restored. Families would be united. Major cities would be eradicated of violence. Deaf ears would be opened. Blind eyes would see. Hungry people would be fed. It would be everything this world witnessed when Jesus was here in flesh and blood, only exponentially multiplied. **Prayer is about transformation.**

In fact, that's what Jesus has in mind for his church to be doing now:

> Very truly I tell you, whoever believes in me will do the works I have been doing, and they will do even greater things than these, because I am going to the Father.[15]

"GIVE US TODAY OUR DAILY BREAD."

Perhaps you may have noticed that up to this point the Lord's Prayer has really concentrated on *the person of God* more than on *the personal*

15 John 14:12

needs of those praying to God. Admittedly, many of my own prayers fall short of this type of vision. Too often, my prayers are focused on myself and my needs from start to finish, which is just one more reason I am thankful for the Lord's Prayer. It draws me out of myself.

In this prayer, Jesus helps us realize that God is so much bigger and greater than our own agenda, needs and wants. When our prayer life focuses mostly on what is wrong in our personal life and how God needs to come and rescue us out of our troubles, we are in serious need of a perspective change. Jesus is teaching us to make the Father, not ourselves or our problems, the focus of our prayers. When we and our problems are the focus of our prayers, it can feel as though God has somehow become smaller, more distant and less powerful. When Father God becomes the focus of our prayer, we quickly discover that it is the size of our problems that becomes smaller.

> *JESUS IS TEACHING US TO MAKE GOD THE FATHER THE FOCUS OF OUR PRAYERS, NOT OURSELVES OR OUR PROBLEMS.*

During my growing-up years, there was a Stroehmann's Bread factory down the street from my home. I could walk by this factory on any given day, and my nostrils would be tantalized by scrumptious scents of fresh-baked bread wafting through the air. It was intoxicating! I don't think I could ever grow tired of that smell.

God the Father loves to provide bread for his children, and it also tastes and smells wonderful. His Word promises: "Taste and see that the LORD is good; blessed is the one who takes refuge in him."[16]

Bread does not just represent physical bread, or even food, but the provision for any need we have in this life. A quintessential example of bread as a provision of God is the manna that God provided divinely each day for the Israelites during the years they wandered in the wilderness. The Israelites were commanded not to hoard, but to gather just enough for each day. This taught them to depend on God for each day's supply.[17]

Similarly, the Christian is instructed in the Lord's Prayer to pray for "daily" bread. The Father wants us to know that he will provide for what

---

16 Psalm 34:8

17 Baker's Evangelical Dictionary of Biblical Theology, "Bread, Bread of Presence", http://www.biblestudytools.com/dictionaries/bakers-evangelical-dictionary/bread-bread-of-presence.html, accessed June 2, 2017.

we need this day and every day. As the apostle Paul expressed in his epistle to the church in Philippi, so it is true for us today: "And my God will meet all your needs according to the riches of his glory in Christ Jesus."[18] Each and every day we wake up, God has provision ready for us, just as he did for the Israelites in the wilderness.

Not only does God want to give us bread to eat, he wants to give us bread that will feed our souls. Father God is in the business of feeding his sheep spiritually as well as physically. When we pray, "Give us this day our daily bread", we are asking God to give us living and fresh words for this day that will provide hope, healing, strength, and encouragement. It is God's will to provide us this spiritual food, which will nourish our inward being, not just our physical bodies. Referring to this type of spiritual nourishment, Jesus told his disciples: "I have food to eat that you know nothing about."[19] **Prayer is about provision.**

"AND FORGIVE US OUR DEBTS, AS WE ALSO HAVE FORGIVEN OUR DEBTORS."

The greatest spiritual need we all have from God is the need of forgiveness. In God's eyes, sin is like a debt that needs to be paid. If you want to get an increase of phone calls at your house, just stop paying your bills for a couple of months. I guarantee you will have collectors giving you a call to collect promptly on their bills. Like a good businessman, Father God will always collect on his debts. But thankfully for each of us, God has taken our entire debt in full and allowed Jesus to pay it on our behalf.

Talk about amazing grace! The next time the pesky devil starts calling you up and hammering you about what you've done wrong, just hand that debt over to the Father and inform your rude debt collector: "Sorry, Satan, you have the wrong number. My Father has paid my account in full with the blood of Jesus." Click. Halleluiah!

It feels good to be forgiven. It feels great to have our guilt and shame taken away. It's like a shower after a long day working in the garden. You can see the dirt and grime swirling down the drain. I love the feeling of a good shower, and I love the feeling of forgiveness by God. How sweet

18 2 Corinthians 12:9
19 John 4:32

it is! "If we confess our sins, he is faithful and just and will forgive us our sins and purify us from all unrighteousness." 1 John 1:9

God's desire is for us to enjoy *giving* forgiveness as much as we do *receiving* forgiveness. In fact, Jesus taught that if we have a grievance between ourselves and another brother or sister in the family of God, it is better to settle our agreement before we even enter into the house of God for worship:

> *Therefore, if you are offering your gift at the altar and there remember that your brother or sister has something against you, leave your gift there in front of the altar. First go and be reconciled to them; then come and offer your gift.*[20]

Jesus tells a story of a man who was forgiven a great debt. Moments after receiving his pardon, this man went looking for a guy who owed him only a fraction of the money he himself had just been forgiven. When he found his debtor, he grabbed him by the throat demanding repayment.[21] Every time we refuse to freely forgive our brothers and sisters from the heart, we are committing the same sin as the man in this parable. When it comes to pardoning our sins, the Father is liberal with his offer to forgive. But he expects us to be just as free in our forgiving of others their sins. **Prayer is about forgiveness.**

"AND LEAD US NOT INTO TEMPTATION, BUT DELIVER US FROM THE EVIL ONE."

Jesus taught us not only to pray for Father God to forgive our sins, but to keep us from the power of sin. In other words, God hasn't made us to be spiritual punch bags that just keep getting hit time and time again with the same blows from the world. Instead, he wants to teach us how to bob and weave so we can avoid taking spiritual upper cuts from the evil one, Satan. The Bible is abundantly clear that God is never out to tempt us to sin. In his New Testament epistle, James wrote:

JESUS TAUGHT US NOT ONLY TO PRAY FOR GOD TO FORGIVE OUR SINS, BUT TO KEEP US FROM THE POWER OF SIN.

---

20 Matthew 5:24
21 See Matthew 18:21-35

When tempted, no one should say, "God is tempting me." For God cannot be tempted by evil, nor does he tempt anyone; but each person is tempted when they are dragged away by their own evil desire and enticed.[22]

God is not our enemy. He is not out to make life harder than it already is for us. In fact, God promises to provide a way to avoid every temptation:

No temptation has overtaken you except what is common to mankind. And God is faithful; he will not let you be tempted beyond what you can bear. But when you are tempted, he will also provide a way out so that you can endure it.[23]

If God would never tempt us to sin, then why would we need to ask God to "lead us not into temptation"? Good question! In case you haven't noticed, the world we live in is full of enticements. We all have our own battles with sin and personal vices. Whether it is lust, greed, idolatry, selfishness, no one is without temptation. Jesus recognized this better than anyone else because he was "tempted in every way, yet without sin."[24]

Jesus is *not* suggesting that God has a tendency to lead us astray. Instead, Jesus knows that we have our own tendencies to fall for the trap of sin and he is instructing us to ask Our Good Father for help in avoiding such failures.

In other words, knowing our own vulnerabilities and weaknesses from his own experience while on this earth, Jesus is teaching us to ask God for help in avoiding the allurement of sins that surround us. We are not asking Father God to stop tempting us, but rather to keep us far away as possible from the sins that beset us. Asking God to keep us from temptation means it is also our responsibility to do our own part by avoiding sin at all costs.

Furthermore, Jesus knows we have an enemy who seeks to knock us out like a Mike Tyson hook to the jaw. If it weren't for our all-powerful heavenly Father and our Big Brother Jesus, we'd be mincemeat for Satan, the world's biggest bully. As the apostle Paul once assured the

---

22 James 1:13-14
23 1 Corinthians 10:13
24 Hebrews 4:15

early Christians facing similar spiritual combat: "But thanks be to God! He gives us the victory through our Lord Jesus Christ."[25] **Prayer is about combat.**

"FOR YOURS IS THE KINGDOM AND THE POWER AND THE GLORY FOREVER. AMEN."[26]

At the end of the day and more critically at the end of our lives, everything goes back to God. Or as the title of the pastor and author John Ortberg's books expresses: *When the Game is Over, It All Goes Back in the Box*. Our lives from beginning to end are encapsulated by God. He is the beginning and the end, the first and the last.[27]

If our lives and our prayers are to make the greatest legacy possible, we must make sure they are directed to the glory and praise of God. As the psalmist said:

> Know that the LORD is God. **It is he who made us, and we are his**; we are his people, the sheep of his pasture.[28]

Everything came from God, and everything will go back to God. Our lives as well as our prayers must begin and end with the Father and his glory in mind. **Prayer is about God's glory.**

Points to Remember:

- Prayer is about community.
- Prayer is about family.
- Prayer is about reverence.
- Prayer is about worship.
- Prayer is about surrender.
- Prayer is about transformation.
- Prayer is about provision.
- Prayer is about forgiveness.
- Prayer is about combat.
- Prayer is about God's glory.

---

25 1 Corinthians 15:57
26 NU omits this portion of the prayer.
27 Revelation 22:13, KJV
28 Psalm 100:3, bold added

Prayer:

"Our Father in heaven, hallowed be your name, your kingdom come, your will be done, on earth as it is in heaven. Give us today our daily bread. And forgive us our debts, as we also have forgiven our debtors. And lead us not into temptation, but deliver us from the evil one. For yours is the kingdom and the power and the glory forever. Amen."

Meditation:

Our Good Father is in Heaven.

Group Discussion:

- Which of the above points to remember do you most relate to and regularly practice in prayer?
- Which of these aspects of prayer would you like to incorporate more regularly in your prayer life?
- If you were asked by someone what it means to pray, how would you respond?
- How would you like to see your own prayer life develop and grow?

Dig Deeper:

Take time to pray slowly through the Lord's Prayer, giving thought to each word and phrase.

CHAPTER NINE

THE UNIVERSAL GOODNESS OF GOD

*"God gives out good gifts of wisdom, talent, beauty,
and skill 'graciously'--that is, in a completely unmerited way.
He casts them across all humanity, regardless of religious
conviction, race, gender, or any other attribute to enrich,
brighten, and preserve the world."*

— TIMOTHY J. KELLER

Alan, a member of our church who has a real heart for God's people, came up to me at the end of a church service one Sunday morning to tell me about an interesting experience he'd had the week prior. He explained, "I had this old basketball hoop. My kids hadn't used it in years, and it wasn't in the greatest shape."

In actuality, the hoop was still in usable condition, but it was slightly bent and had some obvious signs of wear and tear. Alan went on, "At first, I was going to sell it. I figured I could get fifty bucks for it, seventy at best. Then I had a thought. Why not just give this thing away to someone who could use it?"

So Alan took a photo of the hoop, then went onto the local Craigslist website and uploaded the photo under the free section. Within minutes he had received a response from a man in Philadelphia who was interested in acquiring the hoop.

Although the man's initial response was quick, his pick-up of the hoop was much slower. A couple of days later, the man had not yet come to take possession of his "new" hoop. Meanwhile, Alan had received several other requests for the hand-me-down hoop, including one from a local church youth group. Alan explained, "The first guy kept corresponding with me to say he really wanted the hoop, and I wanted to honor him with it since he was the first to respond."

The original caller finally showed up some days later in quite a nice vehicle to pick up the free portable basketball unit. When Alan saw the luxury car pull in, he was sure he had made the wrong decision. With more than a mild sense of guilt, he thought, "Maybe I should have given it to that youth group." The week Alan told me this story I was meditating on the following words from Jesus:

> You have heard that it was said, "You shall love your neighbor and hate your enemy." But I say to you, love your enemies, bless those who curse you, do good to those who hate you, and pray for those who spitefully use you and persecute you, that you may be sons of your Father in heaven; for he makes his sun rise on the evil and on the good, and sends rain on the just and on the unjust. For if you love those who love you, what reward have you? Do not even the tax collectors do the same? And if you greet your brethren only, what do you do more than others? Do not even the tax collectors do so? Therefore you shall be perfect, just as your Father in heaven is perfect.[1]

Jesus is instructing his followers here how to live their lives and pattern themselves after his teachings and life example. So when Jesus makes such statements as "You have heard that it was said", he is laying down a new precedent for his followers that in some way contradicts or overrides their previous understanding of living for God.

Theologian Albert Barnes gives insight into Jesus' teaching on loving our enemies. He states, "The command to love our neighbor was a law of God (Leviticus 19:18). That we must, therefore, hate our enemies was an inference drawn from it by the Jews."[2] Prior to Jesus, it was assumed among his own Jewish disciples that loving our neighbor means we are to do the opposite to those we hate or who hate us.

---

1   Matthew 5:43-48
2   Albert Barnes Notes on the Bible

To love one's neighbor sounds beautiful, poetic, and harmonious. Be good to Mrs. Campbell across the street. She's elderly, but precious in God's sight. Make sure to love Mrs. Campbell. Help her cross the road. Take out her trash for her. Keep watch over her house while she is away. Be good to your neighbor, Mrs. Campbell.

Loving one's neighbor sounds like a noble idea for all of us to practice, don't you think? But Jesus didn't stop there; instead he goes on to instruct: "But I say to you, love your enemies."

Pay attention because Jesus is now setting the new precedent for his followers. According to Jesus' teachings, we are not only to love sweet Mrs. Campbell, the old woman across the street. We are also to love the kids who vandalized her house. We are even to love the man who tried to rob Mrs. Campbell's life retirement savings through a Ponzi scheme. Not to mention the love we are to have for Mrs. Campbell's deadbeat children who have all but neglected their widowed old mother and are waiting to cash in on their inheritance.

WORDS, DEEDS, PRAYERS

Jesus gives us three ways in which we are to love our enemies. The first is with our tongue: "Bless those who curse you." In essence, Jesus is teaching us to say good things to those who say bad things about us. How about that for some divine highway etiquette!

The second is with our hands: "Do good to those who hate you." Jesus is telling us to do good things to people who do bad things to us. Now that's a good New Year's resolution to work on!

Thirdly, Jesus teaches: "Pray for those who spitefully use you and persecute you." If people are spiritually wicked, do not return their wickedness back on them and curse them. Instead we are to pray for them to find God's mercy as we ourselves have found mercy. Lord, give us strength!

The interesting thing about Jesus' teachings in this passage is that each of these responses is contrary to the natural response we have when someone maligns us. If we overhear someone gossiping about us as we approach the coffee room at work, what is our natural reaction going to be? I doubt we'll be thinking about all the nice things we could say about the person criticizing us: "Hmm ... let me see what kind words I can share about her in return." Likewise, if someone hurts us physically, what would our natural response be? Would we be thinking about giving them a foot massage? I think not!

HARD TO BELIEVE STORY

Just a few weeks ago, I went to visit a young girl from our church who had received a kidney transplant. The hospital was in downtown Philadelphia in an area unfamiliar to me. Finding a parking spot in the narrow parking lot, I parked my car there, entered the building and made my way up to the nineteenth floor of this inner-city skyscraper hospital to make my visit. I need to add "the invention of elevators" to my gratitude journal.

Before I left the hospital, I had my parking ticket validated by the security guard on the bottom floor, then paid the reduced-price fee for hospital visitors at a ticket payment machine located near the building's exit. Heading back into the parking lot, I hopped into my faithful, but rather time-battered Toyota Camry and headed to the parking lot's single exit gate.

As I approached the gate, I noticed a car positioned in front of the gate and not moving. There were no attendants waiting to take payments. The only thing that would raise the long bar blocking the exit was a machine that was awaiting an already punched and paid-for ticket. I honked a couple times with a very polite pastoral type of honk: "Beep! Beep! Please move on, dear Mrs. Campbell or whoever you are. I've got places to go."

The car at the gate still did not budge. By now it was blocking not only my own car, but a line of other cars that had pulled up behind me to exit the parking lot. As I waited, I peered ahead into the other vehicle, where I could make out the shadowy forms of two people. They seemed to be carrying on a back-and-forth conversation as though oblivious to the fact that their vehicle was blocking the one and only exit. My initial thought was to get out of my car and go tap on the other vehicle's window just to make them aware of the obvious: "Excuse me, not to state the obvious, but do you realize you are blocking the only and only exit in this parking lot?"

But as I was about to unbuckle my seat belt, an internal voice persuaded me not to venture out of my car to confront the gate blockers. I wasn't sure if this hunch came from the Holy Spirit or was triggered by memories of a scary scene from an old horror movie. I decided to follow my instincts and avoid approaching the car. Instead, I pulled out of the line-up of cars now behind me, backing up carefully through the narrow lot into my previous parking spot. I then got out of the car and walked back to the security guard's station where my ticket had been validated. I figured that I would let the security guard on duty earn his paycheck and handle the situation himself.

As I approached the young guard to tell him my story, I saw that he was already in conversation with a tall man, probably six foot, four inches in height. This tall guy had a sizable gash on his forehead, and blood was slowly trickling down. As I listened to the conversation, I learned that the tall man with the punctured forehead had made the mistake of walking up to the vehicle that was parked in front of the gate. When he did, the lady in the driver's seat had whacked him on the head with her set of keys creating a gash on his forehead. So much for Philadelphia being the city of brotherly love!

At that moment, I realized my decision not to confront the people in the vehicle was probably a wise one and the voice I was hearing in my head was most likely the kind whisper of the Holy Spirit. Meanwhile, the guy who had been assaulted wanted full revenge. He was ready to file a complaint and wanted the security guard to take down every fact.

And who can blame the guy, right? I mean after all, that could have been me! And if it were me, I am sure anyone reading this would want the full extent of the law to be carried out against that angry woman, right? I mean, we have come along far enough in this book that I can consider you my friend now, can't I? And you know what friends do. We stick together. We fight each other's causes. We watch each other's backs. We insist on justice for our friends.

In fact, when we look at our own everyday lives and unjust situations like the one I just described, the words of Jesus become all the more difficult to apply. I mean, just look at what else Jesus had to say on this topic:

You have heard that it was said, "Eye for eye, and tooth for tooth." But I tell you, do not resist an evil person. If anyone slaps you on the right cheek, turn to them the other cheek also. And if anyone wants to sue you and take your shirt, hand over your coat as well. If anyone forces you to go one mile, go with them two miles. Give to the one who asks you, and do not turn away from the one who wants to borrow from you.[3]

Just like the guy with the gash in his forehead, our natural instinct is to react, retaliate, seek revenge, or be resentful. Will we pray for people who spitefully use us? Sure, we will! We will pray that they receive what they deserve and that the law of the land doles out full justice to our offender. Off with their head! Or at least, we'll pray that God gives us justice for our bleeding forehead. In fact, when I actually did offer to pray for the guy who was assaulted, I found myself instinctively praying for justice to prevail in his situation.

If our natural response is to seek justice in this world for the ills of our society, why on earth does Jesus teach us instead to bless, do good, and pray for those who do us wrong? His answer is simple: "that you may be sons of your Father in heaven". The reason Jesus wants us to do good to those who do us wrong is so that we can show the world what it looks like to be a son or daughter of God.

> THE REASON JESUS WANTS US TO DO GOOD TO THOSE WHO DO US WRONG IS SO THAT WE CAN SHOW THE WORLD WHAT IT LOOKS LIKE TO BE A SON OR DAUGHTER OF GOD.

Have you ever seen a son who looks just like his dad or a daughter who looks just like her mother? Jesus is telling us that when we do good to people who do bad to us, we show people what God the Father looks like. We are giving people a picture of Our Good Father that is tangible, real, and life-changing. Jesus explains further: "for he [God] makes his sun rise on the evil and on the good, and sends rain on the just and the unjust."[4]

Jesus spoke these words to people living in an agricultural society. The sun was not just a means of having a nice vacation and gaining

---

3   Matthew 5:38-42
4   Matthew 5:45

the perfectly bronzed skin tone. Sun was essential to growth of one's crops and harvest of one's bounty. So when Jesus says that his Father allows the sun to rise on the evil, he is teaching us that God the Father is good to all mankind and allows everyone to benefit from his kindness. The godly farmer and the wicked farmer next door both delight when the sun shines on their crops, and God is happy to provide sunshine to both parties.

And what about the rain? For the longest time, I thought that when Jesus spoke of the rain, he was saying that God also knows how to allow the natural evils of this life to interfere with both good people and bad people alike. After all, whenever I hear it's going to rain, to me as a suburbanite that is generally bad news. What I forgot was that to an agriculturally-minded audience, rain was a good thing, not bad. Without rain, there would be no crops. So when Jesus told of his Father providing rain for the just and unjust, he was reinforcing the same truth of God's goodness. To send rain on both the God-fearing man's crops and the evil man's crops is a way for God to show his kindness universally to all.

> **GOD THE FATHER IS UNCONDITIONALLY AND UNIVERSALLY KIND TO ALL MANKIND!**

That is the truth we all must grasp. God the Father is unconditionally and universally kind to all mankind. God is good to the man who received the free basketball hoop, and God is good to my God-loving friend Alan. God is good to the woman who struck the man in the parking lot, and God is good to the man who got struck. God is good to the man who praises him on Sunday morning as well as to the guy who uses his Son's name in vain on Sunday afternoon while watching a football game. As phrased in the Bible's longest chapter, Psalm 119: "You are good and do only good; teach me your decrees." [5]

God's goodness is unconditional. He does not play favorites when it comes to his general goodness being shed abroad to all mankind. He allows everyone to receive both sun and rain. He allows all of us to eat, drink, sleep, work, play, and enjoy our lives.

Theologians have a name for this special gift of God to all humanity.

---

5   Psalm 119:68, NLT

It is called "common grace". Common grace is the goodness of God expressed to all humanity, to the sinners and the saints, to the rich and the poor, to the kind and the evil. Common grace includes things like good health, family, children, gifts, talents, abilities, intelligence, laughter, happiness, food, clothes, shelter, sexuality, work, the sun and rain. Every person who lives on this earth has the privilege of experiencing God's common grace when they breathe in the air, smell the flowers, or walk the dog down the street. James, author of the New Testament epistle by the same name, puts it this way:

> Every good and perfect gift is from above, coming down from the Father of the heavenly lights, who does not change like shifting shadows.[6]

James is telling us that everything we see on God's green earth that is good and delightful finds its source from Our Good Father. He is the one who is universally good to all mankind. How awesome! James Merritt writes:

> Contrary to much popular thinking, I don't believe that goodness can possibly exist or be known apart from God. If any meaningful standard determines whether something is good, it must be a universal standard; otherwise, goodness is a matter of opinion...A universal standard of goodness can be determined only by One who is universally good, and that One can only be God. The very word good comes from an Old English word with the same connotation as God. Good-bye is an abbreviation of the phrase, "God be with ye." The word good literally means "to be like God." The word itself implies that when godliness declines, so does goodness.[7]

UNIVERSAL GOODNESS VS. UNIVERSALISM

We must be careful to understand what is meant by the Universal Goodness of God and be sure not to confuse it with a teaching called Universalism, or Universal Salvation. When I state that God is universally good to all mankind, what I am saying is that God the Father

---

6   James 1:17

7   James Merritt, *How to Impact and Influence Others* (Harvest House Publishers, 2011) 96, 97.

enjoys being good to all his creation regardless of their race, creed, color, or religion.

Today, Hindu, Buddhist, Muslim, Christian, and atheist neighbors will all breathe in the same air, no favors being played, because God is universally good to all people. Our Good Father will allow people who deny or misrepresent him to prosper and do well because God is never out to destroy, but to redeem, restore, and save that which is lost. The ill will of man cannot stop the goodness of God.

OUR GOOD FATHER WILL ALLOW PEOPLE WHO DENY HIM TO PROSPER AND DO WELL IN LIFE BECAUSE GOD IS NEVER OUT TO DESTROY, BUT TO REDEEM, RESTORE, AND SAVE THAT WHICH IS LOST.

This is the universal goodness of God. The universal goodness of God does not mean that salvation is universal to all mankind. Universal Salvation states that all people will go to heaven and inherit eternal life, not because they have placed their faith in the God's Son, the Savior, Jesus Christ, but because God is loving, kind, and merciful to all. The Christian Universalist Association statement of faith puts it this way:

> We believe in the full and final triumph of the grace of God over the powers of sin and death: that the mercy and forgiveness of God are victorious; that this victory of redemption is revealed in the life, death and resurrection of Jesus; and that, therefore, **no human being will be condemned or allowed to suffer pain and separation forever.**[8]

God's universal goodness was demonstrated when Jesus died on the cross for the sins of all mankind: "And he **died for all**, that those who live should no longer live for themselves but for him who died for them and was raised again."[9] Jesus' death on the cross is proof that God loved the entire world: "For God so loved the world that he gave his one and only Son, **that whoever believes in him** shall not perish but

JESUS CHRIST IS THE QUINTESSENTIAL EXPRESSION OF GOD'S UNIVERSAL GOODNESS TO ALL MANKIND.

---

8 http://www.christianuniversalist.org/about/beliefs/

9 2 Corinthians 5:15

have eternal life."[10] Jesus Christ is the quintessential expression of God's universal goodness to all mankind.

The question is not and never will be about God's love for humanity. God loves everyone and has demonstrated his love through his son, Jesus Christ. The side of the equation that is missed by those who hold to a belief in universal salvation is that of humanity. God loved us enough to send Jesus to die on the cross for our sins. But we each must accept Jesus' payment for our sins in order to inherit the salvation Jesus paid for with his blood.

The Father loves everyone, so he sent Jesus as a divine "life preserver" that all of humanity can grab hold of him by faith and avoid perishing in the waves of their own sin and rebellion. But we in turn must take action by grabbing hold of that "life preserver": "Yet to **all who did receive him [Jesus]**, to those who believed in his name, he gave the right to become children of God."[11]

God's goodness is unconditionally promised to all, but our salvation is conditionally received by those who accept God's son Jesus as their Lord and Savior. It is kind of like the weekly circular ads my neighborhood receives in the mail. Every household receives the same coupons, but only those who act on the offers benefit from the savings.

---

10 John 3:16
11 John 1:12

Figure 3:

Universal Salvation	Biblical Truth
All people have inherent worth and value and are therefore accepted by God.	All people have inherent worth and value, but all have sinned and need salvation.
All people will be saved because God is merciful.	All who repent and believe in Jesus will be saved.
God's divine love and mercy will reconcile us to himself.	God's divine mercy provided Jesus to pay for our sins in full.
No one will suffer eternally in hell.	Hell is a real place, where real people will go for eternity.

MORE THAN A TAX COLLECTOR

Jesus went on to drive his point home concerning the goodness of God and our lives:

> For if you love those who love you, what reward have you? Do not even the tax collectors do the same? And if you greet your brethren only, what do you do more than others? Do not even the tax collectors do so?

Jesus was making his point clear: "If you want to be seen as my disciples, you must do more than what is expected and customary from everyday citizens." In fact, Jesus said that even a tax collector, a person who was seen as a social crook in his day, knew how to be kind to his own loved ones. Substitute tax collector for unscrupulous lawyer, corrupt politician, or difficult in-laws, and you might be able to relate better to what Jesus was saying.

As believers in Jesus, we may be tempted to look down our spiritual noses at those who do not yet express faith in Christ. Yet the honest truth is that Jesus is not comparing us with those people. In fact, his standard for a follower of Christ is vastly higher than what he expects of unbelievers because we have so much more knowledge, power and grace through his Spirit to show his goodness to the world. "His divine power has given us everything we need for a godly life through our knowledge of him who called us by his own glory and goodness."[12]

Our love should supersede any love demonstrated by people who do not even know Christ as Savior. And here's how. We are not only to care for our neighbors, friends, family members, and those who are nearest and dearest to our hearts, including our neighbor Mrs. Campbell across the street. We are to show God's unmerited, unexplainable, unjustified love and grace to every person we meet, both sinner and saint.

WHEN JESUS TELLS US TO BE PERFECT LIKE THE FATHER, HE IS TEACHING US TO BE PERFECT IN LOVE, NOT PERFECT IN OBEYING ALL THE RULES, BOTH SOCIAL, POLITICAL, AND RELIGIOUS.

Take the parable Jesus told of the Good Samaritan, for instance.[13] A Jewish traveler from Jerusalem to Jericho is beaten up by thieves and left for dead. Two religious guys—a priest and a Levite—pass by without bothering to help the poor victim. In the end it is a Samaritan, who were half-breed Jews despised by full Jews, who stops to rescue the victim.

As he tells the story, Jesus is not criticizing the "foreign" Samaritan, but the two religious Jews who passed by their countryman in need and found themselves too busy to stop and help. How often do we express good and kind gestures to those in church and in our families, yet pass by strangers in need? Jesus concludes: "Therefore you shall be perfect, just as your Father in heaven is perfect."[14]

Be perfect? Oh no, this is not a call to perfectionism, is it? No, it's not, not even close. Instead when Jesus tells us to be perfect like the Father, he is teaching us to be **perfect in love**, not perfect in obeying all the rules, social, political, and religious. "For the entire law is fulfilled in keeping this one command: "Love your neighbor as yourself."[15] God the Father demonstrates his perfect love by allowing the sun to shine and the rain to pour down on both good and bad people. God is calling us to live out the same unconditional love toward mankind.

---

12 2 Peter 1:3
13 Luke 10:25-37
14 Matthew 5:48
15 Galatians 5:14

Going back to my original story of my friend Alan and his basketball hoop, a couple of days after the man had picked up the hoop, Alan received a picture from him in an email. The picture showed the man's young son shooting a basketball through the hoop, now mounted outside a rundown apartment building in Philadelphia. In the body of the email, the man explained how much joy the hoop had brought to his son. One look at the boy's face as he shot the ball through that slightly bent rim brought a smile to Alan's face. He was so glad he hadn't tried to sell this hoop for the mere fifty or seventy bucks it might have been worth because the happiness he'd brought to one little boy from Philly was priceless.

As for the parking lot story, it did not end as triumphantly. The security guard, the injured man and I walked out of the building to take note of the car's license plate so we could report it to the police. By the time we arrived, the car was gone. The assailants had lifted the bar so as to leave the parking lot without paying the fee and escape before law enforcement arrived.

If we make it our goal to always see justice served in this life, we may find ourselves disappointed. Justice is not always served. People do not always receive the due penalty for their wrongs. But then again, neither did we. As children of our gracious heavenly Father, our goal is not to keep score of everyone's wrongs and seek retaliation in return. Instead, it is to show undeserved mercy, goodness and forgiveness, even to those who do not deserve it so as to reflect the kindness of our gracious and merciful Heavenly Father. Consider these scripture commands:

- "Do not repay evil with evil or insult with insult. On the contrary, repay evil with blessing, because to this you were called so that you may inherit a blessing."[16]
- "So speak and so act as those who are to be judged under the law of liberty. For judgment is without mercy to one who has shown no mercy. Mercy triumphs over judgment."[17]
- "He has shown you, O mortal, what is good. And what does the LORD require of you? To act justly and to love mercy and to walk humbly with your God."[18]

---

16 1 Peter 3:9
17 James 2:12-13, ESV
18 Micah 6:8

Each and every day, when the Father tells the sun to shine, the stars to sparkle, the ocean to crash against the shore, and the wind to blow kindly on the face of all mankind, he smiles and is pleased. Why? Because God loves to do good to all mankind. And so should we. As the apostle Paul reminds us: "Therefore, as we have opportunity, let us **do good to all people**, especially to those who belong to the family of believers."[19]

Points to Remember:

- The reason Jesus wants us to do good to those who do us wrong is so that we can show the world what it looks like to be a son or daughter of God.
- God the Father is unconditionally and universally kind to all mankind.
- Jesus Christ is the quintessential expression of God's universal goodness to all mankind.
- God wants us to show his unconditional kindness to all mankind.

Prayer:

"Good Father, thank you for being good, kind and merciful to all mankind."

Meditation:

God is universally good.

Group Discussion:

- What do you feel about God's goodness to unbelievers, even to those who reject him?
- What would it require of you to demonstrate goodness to someone who did you wrong?
- What do you think could be the ramifications if God's people all around the world began to show the goodness of God intentionally and indiscriminately to all mankind?

---

19 Galatians 6:10

Dig Deeper:

Read through the following verses to study more about God's universal goodness.

- Matthew 5:43-48: You have heard that it was said, "You shall love your neighbor and hate your enemy." But I say to you, love your enemies, bless those who curse you, do good to those who hate you, and pray for those who spitefully use you and persecute you, that you may be sons of your Father in heaven; for he makes his sun rise on the evil and on the good, and sends rain on the just and on the unjust. For if you love those who love you, what reward have you? Do not even the tax collectors do the same? And if you greet your brethren only, what do you do more than others? Do not even the tax collectors do so? Therefore you shall be perfect, just as your Father in heaven is perfect.
- Galatians 6:10: Therefore, as we have opportunity, let us do good to all people, especially to those who belong to the family of believers.
- 1 Peter 3:9: Do not repay evil with evil or insult with insult. On the contrary, repay evil with blessing, because to this you were called so that you may inherit a blessing.
- James 2:12-13: So speak and so act as those who are to be judged under the law of liberty. For judgment is without mercy to one who has shown no mercy. Mercy triumphs over judgment.
- Micah 6:8: He has shown you, O mortal, what is good. And what does the LORD require of you? To act justly and to love mercy and to walk humbly with your God.

CHAPTER TEN

You're Not My Daddy!

"One missing child is one too many."

— JOHN WALSH

She's a wild woman. Her two braided pigtails stick out on either side of her head like rabbit ears on an old-fashioned television. Her green, yellow, and red apparel works like a traffic signal to direct her audience's attention. Her dancing, laughing, and various hand gestures are akin to a female version of Pee Wee Herman. She has a strange ability to keep kids as mesmerized to her core message as though watching a Disney movie.

If you don't know who I'm referring to, her name is Angela Shelton, better known as Safe Side Super Chick. She is the star of an Emmy Award winning video series that helps communicate a message of safety to children. One of the show's creators is John Walsh, better known as the host of the TV series *America's Most Wanted*. John is passionate about keeping kids safe from predators and hunting down criminals. This passion was birthed out of a great loss in Walsh's own life. His son Adam was abducted at the age of six and later found dead. After this heartbreaking loss, Walsh and his wife became activists on a mission to help prevent such tragedies and bring criminals to justice.

We can catch a glimpse of the heart of our heavenly Father in John's passion. Just as John seeks to prevent children from being abducted by a person who is not their father, so Our Good Father is passionate about keeping his kids safe from the ultimate predator,

Satan. Just as Walsh has employed Safe Side Super Chick to be his spokeswoman for this cause, so has Our Heavenly Father granted Jesus the right to alert humanity of the one who seeks to deceive his children and lead them astray.

ABRAHAM'S CHILDREN

Strangely enough, it was the religious leaders of his day who Jesus found to be the most dangerous advocates of Satan. These Jews prided themselves on being children of Abraham, the man whom God had promised would be the father of many nations. In one of the most intense showdowns recorded in the Bible, Jesus confronts these religious leaders and their understanding of God's nature:

> "I [Jesus] am telling you what I have seen in the Father's presence, and you are doing what you have heard from your father."
>
> "Abraham is our father," they answered.
>
> "If you were Abraham's children," said Jesus, "then you would do what Abraham did. As it is, you are looking for a way to kill me, a man who has told you the truth that I heard from God. Abraham did not do such things. You are doing the works of your own father."
>
> "We are not illegitimate children," they protested. "The only Father we have is God himself."[1]

CHOPPED

I enjoy watching the reality-based TV show *Chopped*. In each episode, four professional chefs compete against one another in a cook-off. The only catch is that they are required to use a bizarre combination of surprise ingredients. For example, how well would you do in preparing a meal comprised of Asian pears, croissants, haricots verts, and rattlesnake meat? That's just one example of the unusual sets of ingredients these chefs are assigned to work with.

The show is quite intense as the cooks race against the clock to prepare a meal that is not only delicious, but also has a professional presentation. Then comes the moment of truth. Like criminals in a

---

1   John 8:38-41, NIV

lineup, the four chefs stand in a row in front of the judges with nothing to hold onto but the hope that they won't get "chopped" from the show. You can feel their sense of insecurity as they listen to the criticism and critique of each individual judge. It's enough to make me wonder how well I might respond to criticism in an area of my own personal expertise or passion.

Jesus' religious contemporaries prided themselves in being children of Abraham and ultimately of God. They were known to eat, breathe, and sleep God, his commandments, and his laws. They were proud of their identity, their inheritance, and their ancestry. Like a judge on *Chopped*, Jesus comes to critique the very thing they take the most pride in—their understanding of God.

As we stated at the start of this book, Jesus makes the audacious claim to not only know the Father, but to be the only means by which the Father is truly revealed. Jesus had a certain sense of "pride" of his own when it came to knowing who God is and what he is like. Now you can just imagine how heated this conversation is going to get between the religious Jews and Jesus as they debate the nature of God the Father:

> Jesus said to them, "If God were your Father, you would love me, for I have come here from God. I have not come on my own; God sent me. Why is my language not clear to you? Because you are unable to hear what I say. You belong to your father, the devil, and you want to carry out your father's desires. He was a murderer from the beginning, not holding to the truth, for there is no truth in him. When he lies, he speaks his native language, for he is a liar and the father of lies. Yet because I tell the truth, you do not believe me! Can any of you prove me guilty of sin? If I am telling the truth, why don't you believe me? Whoever belongs to God hears what God says. The reason you do not hear is that you do not belong to God."[2]

I have to be honest with you. Jesus makes me uncomfortable here. I mean, if I disagree with someone, I have learned that the best way to approach the situation is to avoid telling the other person that they are wrong and I am right. It just doesn't usually get me very far. Instead I try to first hear the other person out and understand where they

---

2   John 8:42-47

are coming from so that I might be able to understand their position. Ideally, once I feel I have listened without interruption to their side of the story, I try to present my own opinion in the hope that they will give my opinion equal credence. That is my style of confronting issues with other people. I do my best to avoid saying things that will undoubtedly cause offense like, "Your dad is the devil!"

YOUR FATHER, THE DEVIL?

Jesus seems to take a different tactic, at least in this scenario. He goes for what I will call the New Jersey highway approach. Now if you have never driven in the state of New Jersey, let me forewarn you; it is a battleground. You better prepare yourself to get honked at, yelled at, and told where you can go because, believe-you-me, it is going to happen! I don't quite know why, but whenever I cross over the border from my state of residence, Pennsylvania, and enter into the land of New Jersey, I feel as though I'm trespassing on someone else's territory. It's as if they see my PA license plate and think, "Let's get him!"

Well, in his own New Jersey style approach, Jesus comes right after these religious leaders and basically tells them they don't know the first thing about God, the one thing they have prided themselves on the most. He tells them that instead of *driving people to God*, they are *driving people from God*. Jesus indicts them on three specific charges:

- Number 1: They do not love Jesus, the one who has come from God.
- Number 2: They are deaf and cannot hear spiritual truth.
- Number 3: They belong to a different father, the devil, and seek to do his will, not God's.

At this point, I think all chances of friendship are pretty much over. Not only does Jesus indict these religious leaders, but he also calls out Satan along with his identity and agenda:

- Number 1: He was a murderer from the beginning.
- Number 2: He does not hold to the truth and has no truth in him.
- Number 3: His native language is lying. He is the father of lies.

SPOTTING THE COUNTERFEIT

One of the keys to identifying counterfeit money is to compare a fake bill to the real thing. The better you know and understand what a genuine hundred-dollar bill looks like, the easier it is to detect a phony one. The greatest way to spot Satan and his lies is to know the heart of the Father. In the light of the Father's presence, all imposters laying claim to the Father's identity are easily exposed. In fact, this is a major reason I have focused the greater part of this book on who God is instead of who God is not.

> *THE GREATEST WAY TO SPOT SATAN AND HIS LIES IS TO KNOW THE HEART OF THE FATHER.*

The time does come when we also need to make clear the signs of a phony counterfeit bill, or in this case "god" with a lower case "g", who comes as an imitation of the real thing. Just as Safe Side Super Chick alerts children of the very real danger of predators, so Jesus alerts his children of the very real danger of Satan and his lies. Here are some of the things Satan wants us to believe about Our Good Father that Jesus exposed as lies:

- God is angry (in general and with you specifically).
- God wants you to feel guilty and shamed.
- God sees you as a sinner.
- God causes sickness to teach you a lesson.
- God is not truly good.
- God is not trustworthy.

IS GOD ANGRY WITH ME?

Let's take a look at each of Satan's lies in turn. Beginning with the lie that **God is angry**, with his children specifically and with the world in general. In truth, the heart of the gospel is God's love, not his anger. Jesus taught, "For **God so loved the world** that he gave his one and only Son, that whoever believes in him shall not perish but have eternal life."[3] It was not God's anger that compelled him to send his son Jesus to this earth or to the cross. It was the love of God that motivated him to allow Jesus to die on the cross for our sins.

---

3   John 3:16, NIV

Let's be straight. God takes no pleasure in sin. Sin is a serious issue with God. If sin were not a serious issue, God would not have required such a painful and radical sacrifice from his only begotten son Jesus.

ONE OF THE REASONS GOD DESPISES SIN IS BECAUSE HE KNOWS HOW DESTRUCTIVE IT IS TO OUR RELATIONSHIPS WITH HIM, OTHERS, AND EVEN WITH OURSELVES.

The devil wants us to think, "God is angry with me." The truth is that God is angry with sin. Do you see the difference? God hates your *sin*, but God loves *you*. One of the reasons God hates sin is because he knows how destructive it is to our relationships with him, others, and even with ourselves. Being a Good Father, he wants to keep us from relational destruction as well as self-destruction. For this reason, God hates sin.

Satan, the father of lies, wants us to believe that God is angry with us because he knows it will keep us from drawing close to the Father. When was the last time you had the urge to be around someone who was angry with you? God's anger is against sin, and he has demonstrated that anger by allowing Jesus to be punished for your sins and mine. Now we can receive God's love without fear of penalty or judgment because Jesus has taken care of our sin debt on the cross.

THE CROSS OF JESUS MAKES ONE THING VERY CLEAR; GOD TRULY LOVES YOU!

So get this straight! God is not angry with you. God really loves you. Make this a declaration today: "God is not angry with me. God loves me." Say it in the shower. Speak it out while you're driving around town. Tell it to yourself until you believe it with your whole heart: "God is not angry with me. God loves me."

And if you need proof, or maybe just a little reminder, look at what Jesus did for you on the cross. The cross of Jesus makes one thing very clear; God truly loves you! "But God demonstrates his own love for us in this: While we were still sinners, Christ died for us."[4]

---

4   Romans 5:8

DOES GOD WANT ME TO FEEL GUILTY AND SHAMEFUL?

The second lie that Satan wants you to believe is closely related to the first: **God wants you to feel guilt and shame about your sins.** Jesus taught that God's love was the primary motivation for sending him into the world as the Savior. He then went on to say, "For God did not send his Son into the world to condemn the world, but to save the world through him."[5]

The purpose by which the Father sent Jesus to the world was to remove the condemnation and guilt caused by our sins, not to make it greater. I know so many people who have been turned away from God and Jesus because their religious upbringing or religious people in their life have portrayed a message of condemnation instead of a message of freedom from guilt and shame.

Jesus did not come to earth to make us feel more guilt, but to help us recognize our true guilt and turn us to God to see it removed by his grace. Religion says that the closer you are to God the guiltier you should feel. The Gospel, or good news, says the opposite. The better we know God, the more we understand that we are completely forgiven and free from all guilt and condemnation. "If our hearts condemn us, we know that God is greater than our hearts, and he knows everything."[6]

> *THE BETTER WE KNOW GOD, THE MORE WE UNDERSTAND THAT WE ARE COMPLETELY FORGIVEN AND FREE FROM ALL GUILT AND CONDEMNATION.*

Satan will actually use religious sounding arguments (and even religious people) for his own purposes to distort our view of God and impact our relationship with him. When we fail and sin, Satan wants us to run from God, not to God. Satan wants our guilt and shame to make us feel like we cannot approach God. Satan is "the accuser of our brothers and sisters, who accuses them before our God day and night".[7]

The gospel is good news because it provides relief from the burden, guilt and shame of sin, not more of it. Our message is not, "Come to God and feel guilty". It is "Come to God to see your guilt and shame

5 John 3:17
6 1 John 3:20
7 Revelation 12:10

removed." That is the paradox of the gospel of grace – the more we recognize our sin, the greater we see our need for a Savior. The more we fall short, the closer God wants us to come to him to find strength and power to overcome our sinful nature.

Father is not afraid of our sin; he has already dealt with it at the cross. Through the finished work of the cross, God wants to remove the power of sin and its consequences of guilt and shame by drawing us closer, not farther, from himself.

DOES GOD SEE ME AS A SINNER?

Let's look next at Satan's third lie: **God sees you as a sinner.** Now I am the father of three of the most amazing children on the planet. Okay, I know I am biased, but that's fine with me. They are my three favorite kids, and I love them with all my heart.

My kids are not perfect. I see their tendencies towards selfishness. Though the sinful nature may be less evident in childhood, it is still not absent. But my first thought when I look at my kids is never "Look at that little sinner." Of course not! What type of father would I be to think in those terms about my kids? Imagine me introducing my kids to a new acquaintance. "Here is Sinner #1. There's Sinner #2. And beside him is Sinner #3. Aren't they cute?"

Instead, when I see my children, I think, "I am so proud of my sons." Or "I love my daughter to pieces." My love for them is so much greater than their ability to understand or perceive. My focus is not on their failures, frailties and weaknesses, but on their strengths!

When it comes to our identity before the Father, many of us have been taught to see ourselves as "sinners". Now I know that I am a sinner. I have sinned. I do sin. I will sin. So in all technical terms, I am a bona fide sinner through and through. Yet, I understand that when the Father looks at me, his first thought is not "sinner". His first thought is "son". Halleluiah!

Satan wants us to see ourselves as sinners because if we see ourselves through this negative lens, we will be more inclined to sin. Contrarily, if we see ourselves as sons and daughters, we will be more inclined to live righteously. Don't believe me? Try this exercise out for a week. Repeat to yourself a hundred times a day: "I am a sinner ... I am a sinner ... I am a sinner ..." See what that does for your mind, heart, emotions, and behavior. Then for the following week, repeat a hundred times a day this phrase: "I am a child of God ... I am a child of God ... I am a child of God ..." Do this until you believe it with all your heart. Then see which exercise helps you better to resist temptation and live righteously.

Once we receive Jesus into our lives, our identity changes immediately from sinner to child of God:

Yet to all who did receive [Jesus], to those who believed in his name, he gave the right to become children of God—children born not of natural descent, nor of human decision or a husband's will, but born of God.[8]

But what about those people who have not yet received Jesus? Are they sinners? Is that how God sees them? Well, again, technically they are sinners. They have sinned and therefore have earned the title of "sinner". But I think a better way to describe them would be prodigal sons and daughters who have not yet come home to the Father. You see, we can define people by who they are, or we can define people by the destiny God has for their lives. We can look at people based on what they have done wrong or how much God loves them. We can label people based on their poor performance, or we can recognize that every person has been created in the image of God and is loved immensely by the Father.

WE CAN DEFINE PEOPLE BY WHO THEY ARE, OR WE CAN DEFINE PEOPLE BY THE DESTINY GOD HAS FOR THEIR LIVES.

This does not change the gospel message of people needing a Savior or the requirement of repentance before God. It just changes the way we tell the story. It shifts the narrative. Am I a sinner who is seeking refuge for my sins, or am I a wayward child who is coming home to my loving Father? While both stories hold true, one focuses on my sin and shortcoming while the other focuses on God's love and his goodness. I choose to focus on the story of God's redemptive love. I encourage you to consider doing the same.

---

8   John 1:12-13, NIV

DOES GOD MAKE PEOPLE SICK TO TEACH THEM A LESSON?

A fourth lie that Satan tells is that **God causes sickness to teach you a lesson.** Now I myself have experienced a variety of sicknesses and maladies in my life. I have had minor aches and pains as well as more serious issues, including heart surgery. Admittedly, there were a lot of lessons I learned from being sick in my life, and I am sure that God was the teacher of those great truths.

That being said, it is not Our Good Father's goal to make people sick just to teach them a lesson. Can God use sickness as an object lesson for his greater purposes in our lives? Absolutely. The theme of my first book *Born to Grow* is how God uses everything in our lives, both good and bad, for his greater good which is to make us like Jesus. But it's an entirely different story to say that our Good Father makes people sick in order to teach them.

This truth is illustrated clearly by Jesus' own words. As Jesus was walking one day with his disciples, they saw a man who was blind. The disciples asked Jesus, "Rabbi, who sinned, this man or his parents, that he was born blind?"[9] Jesus responded, "Neither this man nor his parents sinned ... but this happened so that the works of God might be displayed in him."[10] Jesus then went on to heal the man.

IN ALL OF JESUS TIME ON EARTH WE DO NOT HAVE A SINGLE STORY OF HIM MAKING SOMEONE SICK—NOT EVEN ONE.

The disciples of Jesus had a serious misunderstanding that is common in our day. They emphatically equated a physical problem (blindness) with a spiritual problem (sin).[11] They figured that someone had to really tick God off big time in order for this man to be born blind. Were his parents wretched sinners? Was this guy born with less value and dignity than the normal human being?

9   John 9:2

10   John 9:3

11   It is important to note that at times there is a direct connection between physical ailments and spiritual issues. For example, some people will experience physical pain and even illness when they choose not to forgive others. Even in these cases, God is not for sickness. He wants us to be physically and spiritually whole and well.

In all of Jesus' time on earth, we do not have a single story of him making someone sick—not even one. But he did heal a countless number of people along the journey. With every healing, Jesus was revealing the heart and nature of the Father. The Father's agenda is to heal people, not to make them sick. God wants to help people become whole, not more broken. God wants to redeem, not to destroy.

This particular subject matter is where the father of lies does some of his best work. If you do not know whether your sickness has been sent by God to teach you a lesson or whether it is something God wants to cure, how can you know if you should pray for it to be healed? After all, if it's God's will for you to be sick so that you can learn a lesson, who wants to pray God's will away? And what good would it be to pray against God's will anyway? You'd be fighting an uphill battle with your hands tied behind your back.

Over the course of Jesus' ministry here on earth, he worked hard at not only exposing the devil's lies, but unraveling his works among humanity. The apostle John wrote: "The reason the Son of God appeared was to destroy the devil's work."[12] When Jesus healed the sick, cast out demons, forgave sins, and provided food for the hungry, he was showing people the heart of the Father towards humanity.

Let's make one thing clear. God is pro-healing and anti-sickness. When God created this beautiful world, he did not create it with sickness and disease. The maladies we suffer with and fight through are part of living in a fallen world. It is true that not every person this side of heaven gets healed, even after receiving prayer. But it is equally true that every person Jesus prayed for was healed without exception.[13] And when we look at the life of Jesus, we see the Father's heart and will. Healing is at the heart of the Father.

Furthermore, we won't find one sickness or disease in heaven. Jesus came to show us what heaven looks like and what the Father's heart is for humanity. Jesus taught us to pray for God's kingdom to come and his will to be done on earth. So praying for healing is part of God's will. Sometimes God answers our prayers in this life, other times the prayers are answered in eternity. In either case, do not miss this important point: God is not out to make people sick, but to bring healing

12 1 John 3:8b
13 See Matthew 4:23

and wholeness to every aspect of our lives. In fact, the entire earthly ministry of Jesus was focused on bringing healing and redemption to a world that was spiritually, relationally, physically, mentally and emotionally sick and broken.

IS GOD TRULY GOOD?

With the above lies ringing in our ears, we shouldn't be surprised at Satan's next lie: **God is not truly good.** Satan wants us to believe that God is not good in every sense. He is fine with us believing that God Is partially good, but not entirely good. In contrast, Jesus presents a completely different image of Our Good Father. He says, "Only God is truly good."[14] In other words, God is not only fully good; he is the only one who can claim the title of being entirely good.

Now I'm sure you have heard it said of others: "He's a good guy." Or "She's a good person." I have spoken these words myself on many occasions about other people. But let's be honest. Is there anyone you know who is truly and entirely good? Is there anyone you know who has no moral flaws, has always obeyed God, has never caused anyone else pain, has always been "good" in every sense of the word? Going a step further, do you know of anyone with a morally pure heart and mind?

When Jesus tells us that "only God is truly good", he is saying that only God is without any moral failures. Only God is free from all sin. Only God is free from the guilt of wrongdoing. Only God is perfect in all of his ways. Only God is completely good.

If you want to grow by leaps and bounds in your relationship with God, get one thing settled straight in your heart. *Know* that God is completely good. Life circumstances are not always fair. Things don't always turn out as we had hoped. But at the end of the day, we can find assurance in knowing that God is completely good. James in his epistle goes a step further in teaching us:

Every good and perfect gift is from above, coming down from the Father of the heavenly lights, who does not change like shifting shadows.[15]

That is to say, every good thing in life from the air we breathe to

14 Mark 10:18b NLT
15 James 1:17

the flowers we see on a Spring day, everything good, without exception, comes from God the Father. Laughter is from God. Joy is from God. Good health is from God. Loving family is from God. Good friends are from God. Even financial prosperity is from God.[16] If it's good, it's from God, period! "Taste and see that the LORD is good; blessed is the one who takes refuge in him."[17]

IS GOD COMPLETELY TRUSTWORTHY?

Which brings us to Satan's final lie: **God is not trustworthy.** You see, the reason Satan wants us to believe God is only partially good is so that he can convince us God is only partially trustworthy. And if God is only partially trustworthy, then he is not fully reliable. Jesus taught something very different: "Don't let your hearts be troubled. Trust in God, and trust also in me."[18]

Nothing good ever comes from a lack of trust in God. Fear, worry, and anxiety are the rewards of those who do not fully trust in God. These are some of Satan's most commonly deployed weapons to paralyze and immobilize God's people.

In contrast, those who trust in God are rewarded with peace, joy, hope and power. As the apostle Paul sums up in a benediction prayer: "May the God of hope fill you with all joy and peace as you trust in him, so that you may overflow with hope by the power of the Holy Spirit."[19] It is no wonder that Satan works overtime to make us doubt God's goodness and squelch our desire to trust in him.

Jesus lived a life of complete and utter dependence on God in order to demonstrate to us how we ourselves are to live. Look at

---

16 "Wealth and honor come from you; you are the ruler of all things. In your hands are strength and power to exalt and give strength to all." (1 Chronicles 29:12) Money and wealth are not evil in themselves. It is greed, avarice and other issues of the heart that are evil. You can have a lot of money and still be godly. You can also be broke and be ungodly. The reverse is also true. You can be poor and godly or rich and ungodly. The amount of money you have is not the question, but instead how much money has you!

17 Psalm 34:8

18 John 14:1

19 Romans 15:13

how Jesus responded when Satan tempted him in the wilderness: "It is written: 'Man shall not live on bread alone, but on every word that comes from the mouth of God.'"[20] One of the most effective means by which we can overcome the lies of Satan is to live by God's Word. As we put our trust in God's Word, we will find God to be faithful. As Scripture assures us:

> God is not human, that he should lie, not a human being, that he should change his mind. Does he speak and then not act? Does he promise and not fulfill?[21]

WHO IS YOUR REAL DADDY?

Tonight I will end my writing around 7:45pm and go pick up my kids from a Bible program at a local church. When I dropped them off earlier in the evening, we went through a check-in process. I was given a sticker with a number on it. The same number on my badge is also on a sticker worn by each of my three kids. When I go to pick up my kids, the workers will look to make sure my badge number matches that of my kids. If a parent shows up without their sticker, they will be required to present formal identification.

All this to pick up my own kids!

Honestly, I am thankful for the procedure. I'm even thankful for the occasional times when I get "carded" at the door. I am thankful because I would never in a million years want to suffer the loss of one of my children to a predator. I don't know how John Walsh survived his trauma let alone became a national spokesperson for tracking down criminals. God has awarded that man with some amazing grace!

The next time you hear a whisper in your ear that in any way makes you question the goodness of God Our Father, check that voice against his real identity found in his Word. Remember the words of Jesus: "Only God is good". Then ask yourself: "Is this the voice of my true Father?" The better you know Our Good Father, the quicker you'll be able to recognize the father of lies.

In an episode of her show, Safe Side Super Chick teaches kids to yell out if they are in any danger of abduction: "You're not my dad!

20 Matthew 4:4
21 Numbers 23:19

You're not my mom!". In the same way, Jesus wants us to be aware of the lies Satan speaks about Our Good Father so we can call out: "No! That's not my Good Daddy!"

Points to Remember:
- God is not angry with you. God loves you.
- God wants to remove the feelings of guilt and shame through the work of the cross.
- God sees you as his beloved child, not as a sinner.
- God can use sickness to teach you, but God does not cause sickness to teach you.
- God is the only one who is truly good in every sense of the word.
- God is trustworthy, and we can rely on his Word.

Prayer:
"Good Father, expose every lie that I believe about you."

Meditation:
Satan is a liar. God is always good.

Group Discussion:
- What are some of the motivations that cause a person to tell a lie?
- Which lie discussed in this chapter speaks most directly to you personally?
- How does believing a lie (about God or in any area of life) hurt you?
- How could fully believing God's Word and not doubting change one's life?

Dig Deeper:
Read through the following verses to think about how Jesus describes the devil.
- John 8:44: You belong to your father, the devil, and you want to carry out your father's desires. He was a murderer from the beginning,

not holding to the truth, for there is no truth in him. When he lies, he speaks his native language, for he is a liar and the father of lies.

- John 10:10: The thief comes only to steal and kill and destroy; I have come that they may have life, and have it to the full.
- John 14:30: I will not say much more to you, for the prince of this world is coming. He has no hold over me.

CHAPTER ELEVEN

LOVING DADDY

"Trust in him at all times, you people; pour out your hearts to him, for God is our refuge."

— KING DAVID

Sometime back, I went to the local office supply store to buy some materials for classrooms in our church. While in the store, I found a couple of flipchart easels on sale. I knew we could use them, and the lowered price made it an easy decision. So I took the last two remaining boxes containing the easels and headed to the register with my other items.

When I brought the two boxes back to the church and opened them, I found to my dismay that some important pieces were missing from one of the boxes. First of all, there were no instructions. That was not too much of a problem since my other box had instructions. The bigger problem was that the hardware necessary to put the easel together was missing. I was forced to return this "great deal" to the store.

Maybe you have been reading along in this book and you have been tracking with my message and, more importantly, the words of Jesus about our Father's good nature. You really want to fully embrace Our Good Father for all he is, but you feel like something is missing in this package. Your life experiences, and in particular your disappointments, are hindering you from fully embracing the concept of a "Good Father".

Or maybe it's not your past experiences, but your intellect that is holding you back from embracing a picture of an all good and loving God. You want to be authentic, and you want to believe what is true. So, being the honest, authentic, inquisitive, and intelligent person that you are, you have some deeper questions you want answered like:

- If God is so good, why do I have so much pain in my life?
- If God is good, why do so many people suffer in this world?
- If God is so good and also all powerful and in complete control, why does he allow bad things to happen, especially to good people?

Let me assure you of a couple of things I have learned about God. First of all, he's not afraid or surprised by our questions. In fact, he already knows them. So why not just be honest and direct with him about how we think and feel?

Secondly, he's not upset with us because of our question. God welcomes both the skeptic as well as the scholar to come to him with their sincere inquiries and concerns. He has nothing to fear or hide, and that includes our questions. God is completely secure in who he is and is not disturbed by our doubts and inhibitions.

Thirdly, I have learned that God does not necessarily answer our questions "on demand". Sometimes we get a quick response. Other times we wait. And still other times we may never know the answers we are looking for this side of heaven.

IF JESUS WAS TRULY "TEMPTED IN EVERY WAY" AS WE ARE, THEN HE MUST UNDERSTAND WHAT IT MEANS TO BE TEMPTED TO QUESTION THE GOODNESS OF GOD IN THE MIDST OF ADVERSITY.

When it comes to the above questions about God's goodness in the midst of trials, hardship, and heartbreak, the best answers still come from the person who knows the Father best—his son Jesus. The author of Hebrews describes Jesus' ability to empathize with and understand our questions and life struggles this way:

> For we do not have a high priest [Jesus] who is unable to empathize with our weaknesses, but we have one who has been tempted in every way, just as we are—yet he did not sin.[1]

If Jesus was truly "tempted in *every* way" as we are, then he must understand what it means to be tempted to question the goodness of God in the midst of adversity. Jesus must know what it is like to be

1   Hebrews 4:15

138

in a situation in which there is inconsolable pain, suffering, heartache, and a deep sense of loneliness. Jesus must also understand what it means to question the sovereignty of God, the goodness of God, and even the plan of God for his own life and in the world. If Jesus, the compassionate high priest, was truly tempted in every way humanly possible, then he must understand how we feel when life seems unfair, unjust, and even unbearable.

THE ANGUISH OF JESUS

After the final meal before his death, Jesus took his three closest friends with him to pray:

> They went to a place called Gethsemane, and Jesus said to his disciples, "Sit here while I pray." He took Peter, James and John along with him, and he began to be deeply distressed and troubled. "My soul is overwhelmed with sorrow to the point of death," he said to them. "Stay here and keep watch."[2]

Jesus found himself in the most stressful and anxiety-ridden moment of his earthly existence. In his own account of Jesus' life and death, Luke adds that the anguish Jesus felt was so deep that it caused him to sweat blood. Luke, known as "the beloved physician", is actually describing a rare, but very real, medical condition known as Hematidrosis.[3] The sweat glands are surrounded by tiny blood vessels. Under certain circumstances, these vessels can constrict and then dilate to the point of rupture. The blood will then effuse into the sweat glands, which then actually sweat blood. The instigating cause—extreme anguish.[4]

In this intense and painfully stressful moment, Jesus turns to the one and only person whom he believes he can trust, his Good Father. The scene brings some of the following questions to mind:

- How will Jesus pray when life is crashing down on him?
- How will Jesus address his "Good Father" when life seems anything but good?

2 Mark 14:32, NIV

3 Luke 22:44, NIV

4 Why Did Jesus Sweat Blood in the Garden of Gethsemane?, http://www. gotquestions.org/sweat-blood-Jesus.html, accessed January 21, 2016.

- What will we learn from the prayer of the Son of God in the most vulnerable time of his life?

THE PRAYER OF JESUS

Let's take a look at what and how Jesus prayed:

Going a little farther, he fell to the ground and prayed that if possible the hour might pass from him. "Abba, Father," he said, "everything is possible for you. Take this cup from me. Yet not what I will, but what you will."[5]

First, we see what Jesus does. In a sign of humble submission and desperation, he falls to the ground. He then cries out to God in prayer. For the first and only time recorded in Holy Scripture, Jesus uses the word "Abba" when he addresses his Father. The word Abba is from Aramaic, and it means "Daddy". It is a word young children would use when speaking to their father whom they trust. It is a loving and endearing term, not the type of word you would use with a stern or strict earthly father.

Does it come as a surprise to you that in this moment of extreme emotional turmoil and anxiety Jesus addresses God with the tender and soft word "Abba", meaning "Daddy"? I know it surprised me. But maybe you are thinking, "Well, this is Jesus. Of course he is going to give the perfect response to God. He is God himself!"

NOT ONLY DID JESUS ENDURE PHYSICAL PAIN AND ANGUISH, HIS HUMANITY MADE HIM SUBJECT TO THE WHISPERS OF THE DEVIL, THE DOUBTS OF HIS HUMAN NATURE, AND THE RATIONAL MIND THAT CRIES OUT, "THIS IS JUST NOT FAIR!"

Yes, Jesus is divine. Let us not overlook the fact that Jesus was also fully human. He experienced temptation at the greatest degree and level possible. After all, he was sweating blood at this point. Not only did Jesus endure physical pain and anguish, his humanity made him subject to the whispers of the devil, the doubts of his human nature, and the rational mind that cries out, "This is just not fair!" And yet, under all the pressures to question the goodness of God, Jesus prays, "Daddy".

5   Mark 14:35-36, NIV

After Jesus addresses the Father with the most endearing of sentiments, he acknowledges God's power and sovereignty by stating "everything is possible for you." The word "possible" comes from a Greek word, *dunatos*, which means powerful or capable.[6] Jesus is acknowledging that God has the power to get him out of this situation. In theological terms, Jesus is saying, "God, you are omnipotent and sovereign. You are all-powerful and in complete control. You have all the ability and capacity to completely change my situation."

The deeper meaning of this statement cannot be overlooked. It is in this statement that Jesus is striking at the heart of the question above which so many of us have asked or thought: "If God is so good and also all-powerful and in complete control, why does he allow bad things to happen, especially to good people?"

Jesus is asking God to work on the basis of his power and ability to do the impossible. Jesus submits his prayer request to his Good Father asking him to "take this cup from me". Christian author Dr. Mark D. Roberts, in an article for *The High Calling* magazine, poignantly explains the significance of this statement:

> The cup of Jesus will involve suffering, to be sure. Yet "cup of suffering" doesn't quite get what Jesus meant when he referred to a cup. If we look in the Old Testament, we find that the metaphor of the cup stands for our lives, which can be filled with a variety of things. Our "cup" can be filled with blessing and salvation (Ps. 23:5; 116:13), or it can be filled with wrath and horror (Isa. 51:17; Ezek. 23:33). Frequently, the cup stands for God's judgment and wrath. Consider, for example, Isaiah 51:17: "Wake up, wake up, O Jerusalem! You have drunk the cup of the LORD's fury. You have drunk the cup of terror, tipping out its last drops." Many other Old Testament passages use the metaphor of the cup as a reference to God's fierce judgment.
>
> Thus, when Jesus prays about avoiding the cup, he is alluding to these images from the Scriptures. By going to the cross, he will drink the cup of God's wrath, all the way to the bottom. He will bear divine judgment, that which rightly falls upon Israel and, indeed, upon all humanity. In this process, he will suffer horribly, both in the physical realm and especially

6   Strong's Greek Dictionary #1415

in the spiritual realm as he enters the Hell of separation from his Father.[7]

In full knowledge of the cup the Father is asking him to bear, Jesus says, "Yet not what I will, but what you will." The prayer Jesus taught his disciples to pray— "Thy kingdom come, thy will be done"—is his own heart cry to the Father. He lays his life down in humble submission to do his Father's will, no matter what the cost, trusting his Good Father with the final results. Jesus sums it up this way: "Because of this my Father delights in me, because I am laying down my life that I may receive it again."[8]

Let me take the liberty to paraphrase this passage of Scripture and put it into my own words:

Jesus can't even take another step. He falls to the ground in deep anguish and distress. He finds himself in a surreal moment where time seems to move at an unprecedentedly slow pace. With his face pressed flat against the earth he himself created, he calls out to his Father. "O dear Daddy ... my loving and faithful Daddy ... I know that you can take care of me here. I know that you have all the power in the world to save me from this trial. Please, dearest Father, take away your anger and judgment. Don't make me take this on myself, loving Father. There truly must be a better way. Regardless, Daddy, the one whom I love, I want you to know that I truly trust your decision. Whatever you think is best, I will accept, hands down, no argument. I will do it."

ABANDONED

At this point in the story, I truly wish we could read that the Father responded. It would be a great time to hear the booming voice of Daddy down to his Son. A message of rescue and salvation would be ideal: "Don't worry, my son, I will deliver you." Or maybe a message of hope: "Son, I have a plan that I am working on." Or at least a message of comfort: "My son, my grace will carry you through this situation."

---

7   What is the Cup That Jesus Wants His Father to Take Away?, Mark Roberts, http://www.thehighcalling.org/articles/daily-reflection/what-cup-jesus-wants-his-father-take-away, accessed January 21, 2016.

8   John 10:17, Aramaic Bible in Plain English

Instead, there is silence.

Because of this moment in time, we know that Jesus can relate to the silence we ourselves have experienced. Maybe you've been through such a heart-wrenching situation when you were on bended knee, crying out to God in hopeful

JESUS KNOWS WHAT IT FEELS LIKE TO HAVE HEAVEN ON MUTE WHEN SUFFERING IS ON HIGH.

desperation that you would hear some voice or heavenly message to comfort you.

Instead, there was silence, a deep and long silence. If you have ever faced such painful, silent moments, be assured of this one thing. Jesus knows what it feels like to have heaven on mute when suffering is on high.[9]

YOUR BEST FRIENDS ARE SLEEPING

A last resort for Jesus was bringing his three closest friends and confidants to come alongside him to help support, comfort, console and pray for him in his time of anguish and pain. At least he would not be *totally* alone. If God would not speak up, he could rely on his closest friends to come alongside him, pray for him, comfort him, and show him the compassion and empathy he so desperately needed in this cruel hour. Yet the song of disappointment played once again. Jesus returns to his friends to find them fast asleep! As stated in my book, *Born to Grow*:

> [We] see from Jesus' story, His closest friends failed Him in His greatest moment of weakness. Instead of staying awake with Him and praying as He asked, these guys fell asleep. In the moment when Jesus needed close friends the most, He found Himself alone. Jesus experienced disappointment in relationships.[10]

---

9   To be fair and biblically accurate, it should be noted that the Father had previously spoken to Jesus about the trial he was going to face. See John 12:27-30. In this passage, we see that Jesus willingly accepts the cross as a means of glorifying the Father. We also learn that the Father would glorify Jesus through the cross.

10 *Born to Grow*, Pierre M. Eade, (Xulon 2014) 130, www.borntogrowbook.com.

HOW THE MOVIE ENDS

I remember a time when I went to the movies in Paris, France, to watch a film that was written and produced by people of that culture. Now as an American I have a certain subconscious expectation of every movie: the hero always wins in the end. That's the American dream. If you haven't yet noticed, most movies produced in America end with the winner on top. Which by the way, if you ask me, is the way it should be!

I distinctly remember walking out of the movie theatre in Paris that evening. Women who had watched the film left crying, some even sobbing. Men were frozen in silence, not able to speak a word.

The ending of the film was not a happy one. It was painful. The hero did not come and save the day. Evil had won. And this young American boy was in a haze, thinking, "What did I just experience?" Ending a movie without a triumphant finish was bewildering and upsetting. Somebody made a huge mistake!

But let's be honest for a moment. Not all of life's stories end so pleasantly, do they? Just a few weeks back, I attended a funeral for a young man who had overdosed. I can promise you this was not the "happy ending" his parents had in mind when he was born into this world. Life at times seems to end in more pain than victory.

Jesus' own life ended on what seemed to be a pretty dismal and painful note. A crowd chose to have him executed instead of a convicted murderer. He was mocked, spat upon, and utterly humiliated. He was killed next to two criminals. All but one friend abandoned him as he hung indecently on the cross. The movie of Jesus' life did not end in triumph.

THE SEQUEL

If it were up to me, there would have been a sequel to that movie I saw in France. Yes, there would definitely be a second half of the story. Hope would be restored. Hurts would be healed. Redemption would be realized, and people would walk out of the theater inspired, hopeful, and happy.

In the same way, my heart looks upon this world and cries for some form of redeeming value to all of life's misery and pain. I look to

Abba Father, loving Daddy, and I think, "Good God, you have got to do something about this!" I want to see God's redemption here on earth, not just in heaven. The apostle Paul recognized this heart cry of all creation when he penned these words to the church in Rome:

> I consider that our present sufferings are not worth comparing with the glory that will be revealed in us. For the creation waits in eager expectation for the children of God to be revealed. For the creation was subjected to frustration, not by its own choice, but by the will of the one who subjected it, in hope that the creation itself will be liberated from its bondage to decay and brought into the freedom and glory of the children of God. We know that the whole creation has been groaning as in the pains of childbirth right up to the present time. Not only so, but we ourselves, who have the first fruits of the Spirit, groan inwardly as we wait eagerly for our adoption to sonship, the redemption of our bodies. For in this hope we were saved. But hope that is seen is no hope at all. Who hopes for what they already have? But if we hope for what we do not yet have, we wait for it patiently. [11]

The whole world is eagerly waiting for God's redemption. The whole earth is longing for the sequel to be released. And the good news is this: our present sufferings in this age are not comparable to the amazing, glorious, and bright future we will have with Our Good Father in eternity. The sequel is coming!

The message of the cross is that Our Good Father would allow his very own Son to suffer and die for the redemption of the earth. In Jesus' pain and agony, we find our own redemption and hope. Jesus' death took away the penalty of our sins, but also brings healing to our souls. He died so we can live. He was killed so we can have new life. He was sacrificed so we can be set free. He suffered so we can find relief.

THE SEQUEL IS COMING

Thankfully, Jesus' life did not end on the cross. Three days after Jesus was gruesomely murdered, God brought him back to life. The resurrection of Jesus is God's sequel to the pain and suffering of this

---

11 Romans 8:18-25, NIV

world. And through the resurrection, each of our darkest and most difficult moments can be filled with hopeful expectation. We can know that Our Good Father has a plan to bring about redemption in this world.

The thing you must not forget is that with any suffering is waiting. ❯ Sometimes you only wait a short period of time before your problem is resolved or your healing comes. Other times you may wait years. And in still other cases, you may have to wait until you meet your Redeemer and Healer face-to-face. The author of Hebrews explains the hope we have as people of faith:

> *All these people were still living by faith when they died. They did not receive the things promised; they only saw them and welcomed them from a distance, admitting that they were foreigners and strangers on earth. People who say such things show that they are looking for a country of their own. If they had been thinking of the country they had left, they would have had opportunity to return. Instead, they were longing for a better country—a heavenly one. Therefore God is not ashamed to be called their God, for he has prepared a city for them.* [12]

The Bible is filled with stories of waiting for a sequel to come. Abraham had to wait until his old age before he received the sequel of his promised son. Jacob served seven years for the sequel of his wife Rachel. Joseph waited through betrayal, slavery, imprisonment, and famine before the sequel of his dreams came to fruition. The Jews waited in silence for four hundred years before the sequel of their Messiah's birth. The friends of Jesus waited three long and hopeless days before the sequel of Jesus being resurrected. As the apostle Paul sums up: "But if we hope for what we do not yet have, we wait for it patiently." [13]

❯ Here's my question to you: "What are you waiting for?"

You may be waiting and hoping for your son or daughter to come to Christ. Or you may be waiting for them to break free from an addiction. You may be waiting for your spouse to accept the Lord. You may be waiting for your own healing. You may be waiting for reconciliation between family members. You may be waiting for your calling to be

---

12 Hebrews 11:13-16, NIV
13 Romans 8:25

fulfilled. You may be waiting for a breakthrough in your finances. We are all waiting for something.

If you are still waiting for redemption, healing, answers to the tough questions in life, be assured of this: Our Good Father always has a redemptive plan in the works. The resurrection of Jesus tells us that God is working behind the scenes, weaving his redemptive plans through all of creation and in your life. God is in the process of writing the script for the sequel to your story.

> *GOD IS IN THE PROCESS OF WRITING THE SCRIPT FOR THE SEQUEL TO YOUR STORY.*

While you are waiting, while you are hoping, while you are trusting, while you are praying, just remember Jesus in the garden of Gethsemane. He did not want to go through the suffering or anguish, but he never allowed his pain to remove his confidence in the goodness of God. So when life seems the hardest, your pain runs the deepest, and you feel all alone, remember Jesus' words in the garden and make them your own:

"Loving Daddy, I trust you."

"Loving Daddy, I believe in you."

"Loving Daddy, I put my hope in you."

"Loving Daddy, I seek to honor you."

"Loving Daddy, I want to do your will no matter what."

Points to Remember:

- Jesus was tempted in every way, yet did not sin.
- Jesus knows what it feels like to have heaven on mute when suffering is on high.
- Good Father always has a redemptive plan in the works.

Prayer:

"Loving Daddy, I put my total trust in you. Help me to know your presence and to always do your will."

Meditation:

Father is still good when life is painful.

Group Discussion:

- When have you been most tempted to question the goodness of God?
- How do you feel about calling God "Loving Daddy" in your most difficult times?
- What can you learn from the way in which Jesus endured the suffering of the cross?

Dig Deeper:

Read through the following verses to think more about the sufferings of Jesus and in the world today:

- Hebrews 4:15: For we do not have a high priest (Jesus) who is unable to empathize with our weaknesses, but we have one who has been tempted in every way, just as we are - yet he did not sin.
- Mark 14:35-36: Going a little farther, he fell to the ground and prayed that if possible the hour might pass from him. 'Abba, Father," he said, "everything is possible for you. Take this cup from me. Yet not what I will, but what you will."
- Romans 8:18-25: I consider that our present sufferings are not worth comparing with the glory that will be revealed in us. For the creation waits in eager expectation for the children of God to be revealed. For the creation was subjected to frustration, not by its own choice, but by the will of the one who subjected it, in hope that the creation itself will be liberated from its bondage to decay and brought into the freedom and glory of the children of God. We know that the whole creation has been groaning as in the pains of childbirth right up to the present time. Not only so, but we ourselves, who have the first fruits of the Spirit, groan inwardly as we wait eagerly for our adoption to sonship, the redemption of our bodies. For in this hope we were saved. But hope that is seen is no hope at all. Who hopes for what they already have? But if we hope for what we do not yet have, we wait for it patiently.

CHAPTER TWELVE

Giving God's Goodness Away

"Do all the good you can. By all the means you can. In all the ways you can. In all the places you can. At all the times you can. To all the people you can. As long as you ever can."

— JOHN WESLEY

A letter to the editor of our local newspaper voiced one disgruntled resident's aversion toward the Christian faith. The main argument of the editorial was that the message of Christianity, which points solely to Jesus as the way to salvation, is too restrictive and dogmatic.

To be fair, the author had some well-articulated, logical arguments peppered with some disappointing expressions of the Christian faith he had experienced in his childhood. Reading the article did not incite anger or hostility within me, but a sense of compassion and sorrow for a lost son of the Father who had not yet found his way home.

But what struck me most powerfully as I read the article was not the arguments against the Christian faith. I had heard this line of thinking before and could offer counterarguments to refute his ideology. No, what struck me was the writer's closing remarks to any Christ followers who might be reading his words. After giving the God of the Bible no more credibility than any other purported god or idol, he gave some interesting advice to Christians readers: "I hope

Christians keep the love, peace, and charity aspects of their religion and abandon [their dogmatic beliefs]."[1]

This final comment captivated me for two reasons. First, the writer was clearly aware that Christians are people of good works, generosity, and love. It is quite likely that the author had himself been witness to such benevolence, either as a personal recipient or through his observations of the world around him.

Secondly, even though he strongly disagreed with the **orthodoxy** of Christianity, i.e., the beliefs held by adherents of the faith, he was tolerant of the **orthopraxy** of Christians, i.e., those beliefs put into action.

Interesting isn't it? People who oppose the beliefs of Christianity are not necessarily opposed to the good works accomplished by Christian individuals or the community of faith at large for the betterment of society. Have you ever heard someone complain, "Christians have founded too many hospitals in the world"? Likewise, we would have a hard time finding people who protest against the efforts of Christians to feed and clothe the poor, provide clean drinking water or help women escape sex trafficking.

Conversely, when people hear that we profess faith in God, but then see that our lives and speech do not produce the type of behavior associated with a God-loving person, they become critical of our expressed faith.

A bumper sticker displayed by one of my former neighbors where I used to live said it best: "Your beliefs don't make you a better person, your behavior does." Well said! In his epistle to the early church, James expressed it this way:

> What good is it, my brothers and sisters, if someone claims to have faith but has no deeds? Can such faith save them? Suppose a brother or a sister is without clothes and daily food. If one of you says to them, "Go in peace; keep warm and well fed," but does nothing about their physical needs, what good is it? In the same way, faith by itself, if it is not accompanied by

---

1   "Selling Salvation: The dogma of all or nothing", Bucks County Courier Times, April 13, 2015, Harry M. Woodruff.

action, is dead. But someone will say, "You have faith; I have deeds." Show me your faith without deeds, and I will show you my faith by my deeds. You believe that there is one God. Good! Even the demons believe that—and shudder.[2]

James goes on to give examples of faith in action. He tells of Abraham who at God's command offered his own son Isaac as a sacrifice, believing that God would provide the ultimate sacrifice and spare his son, even if it meant raising Isaac from the dead. Then there is the story of Rahab who in faith hid Israelite spies in her house, saving their lives while risking her own. In fact, throughout the Bible we find people who were imperfect and flawed, but had a genuine faith in God that provoked them to action.

So as we come to know and appreciate the message of God the Father being good, it only makes sense to ask the question: "So now what?"

- Is understanding the goodness of God an end to itself?
- Is there something we are actually called to do?
- How do we apply the goodness of God we have come to understand, appreciate, believe, and receive for ourselves?

Furthermore, what role does our faith play in guiding other people without faith (like the guy who wrote the scathing editorial against Christianity)? According to Jesus, we have been assigned an important task to carry out. Here's what he said about it:

You are the salt of the earth; but if the salt loses its flavor, how shall it be seasoned? It is then good for nothing but to be thrown out and trampled underfoot by men. You are the light of the world. A city that is set on a hill cannot be hidden. Nor do they light a lamp and put it under a basket, but on a lampstand, and it gives light to all who are in the house. Let your light so shine before men, that they may see your good works and glorify your Father in heaven.[3]

SALT OF THE EARTH

In ancient times, salt served a variety of purposes. One purpose we are familiar with today is that salt makes food taste better. But salt doesn't

2 James 2:14-19, NIV
3 Matthew 5:13-16

just make even a drab diet more palatable; it is also necessary to our physical body's good health. Let me explain.

I had been working out consistently during college years and gained some considerable size and strength. One of the football coaches saw me working out in the school's weight room and invited me to join the team. So in my senior year of college, I decided to give the football team a shot and make the most of the opportunity. At the time, I was big into nutrition and loved to learn about the right foods to eat and what was best for our body's nourishment, energy, and strength. Somewhere along the line, I learned that after people work out they tend to want salt on their food. This is because sodium (a key component of salt) is lost through perspiration, producing a need in our bodies for a refill.

The football team was a great litmus test of this truth. After practices, the team would head together to the school's cafeteria to feast and replenish. Let me tell you, football players know how to eat! I can still remember what took place as each player sat down with their tray at a table. Instinctively, the first thing they would do is to grab for the salt shaker and dash a hefty amount of salt on their food. Why? Their sweaty bodies craved salt, and they responded accordingly. Salt was not just making their food taste better. It was actually restoring their health.[4]

In ancient times salt was not just vital for dietary health, it was often used as well for medicinal and healing purposes.[5] Egyptian, Greek and Roman societies used salt for a variety of purposes including drying out wounds, as a laxative, curing digestive issues, healing skin and other diseases.[6]

In the world we live in, life tends to suck the salt out of us. The overall sense of God's goodness can get lost in the midst of hardship, stress, and life's daily annoyances. All of us can at times feel the weariness of living in a world that leaves us feeling dry, especially when we interact with people who are at times "tasteless".

---

4 *Salt for Society*, W. Phillip Keller, page 93.

5 Ibid, page 115.

6 A Taste for Salt in the History of Medicine, Eberhard J. Wormer, http://www.tribunes.com/tribune/sel/worm.htm

Jesus said, "You are the salt of the earth". In other words, we as believers in Christ and Our Good Father, are the salt shaker on the table of this world that allows people to "taste and see that the Lord is good".[7] Our good works provide the taste of God's goodness to a world that is feeling bland or tasteless.

Another vital purpose for salt in ancient times was to preserve. In a time when the modern convenience of refrigeration was not available, salt not only served as a preservative to help foods stay fresh and edible for longer durations of time, but also to prevent and limit the growth of bacteria and mold.[8]

This purpose for salt also aligns well with our purpose as children of Our Good Father in this world. We as a people are called to be a preservative to our culture and generation. You may ask what being a preservative looks like. In actuality, it can take on many forms. But generally speaking, being a preservative requires us to speak up and act on behalf of those who are lost, sick, downtrodden, afflicted, forgotten, marginalized, and mistreated in this world. It is our purpose to preserve the goodness of God against the evils of poverty, injustice, oppression, racism, abuse, discrimination, and any other form of hatred or intolerance. King Solomon in the book of Proverbs sums it up this way:

> *Speak up for those who cannot speak for themselves, for the rights of all who are destitute. Speak up and judge fairly; defend the rights of the poor and needy.*[9]

But Jesus doesn't just tell us that we are to be salt in the world. He goes on to ask a rhetorical question: "If the salt loses its flavor, how shall it be seasoned? It is then good for nothing but to be thrown out and trampled underfoot by men." 19th century theologian and biblical commentator Albert Barnes helps bring understanding to Jesus' words as he describes the difference between the composition of salt in ancient times versus today:

---

7   Psalm 34:8a

8   Why Does Salt Work as a Preservative?, Anne Marie Helmenstine PhD, https://www.thoughtco.com/why-does-salt-work-as-preservative-607428, accessed May 13, 2017.

9   Proverbs 31:8-9

The salt used in this country is a chemical compound-muriate of soda- and if the saltiness were lost, or it were to lose its savour, there would be nothing remaining. It enters into the very nature of the substance. In eastern countries, however, the salt used was impure, mingled with vegetable and earthy substances; so that it might lose the whole of its saltiness, and a considerable quantity of earthy matter remain. This was good for nothing, except that it was used, as it is said, to place in paths, or walks, as we use gravel. This kind of salt is common still in that country. It is found in the earth in veins or layers, and when exposed to the sun and rain, loses its saltiness entirely. [10]

What would it mean for us as believers to "lose our saltiness"? Losing one's saltiness is not about losing our salvation or our faith in Christ. It is about becoming so much like the world that our lives are no different, not distinct in any manner, from the neighbor next door who lives his life apart from faith in the Father or his beloved Son Jesus. It is living a life that is in pursuit of our own satisfaction and earthly pleasure instead of living a life filled with good works, deeds, and action for the good of others. It is a life centered around building our personal kingdom instead of one focused on advancing the kingdom of heaven here on earth.

LIGHT OF THE WORLD

As I sit at my kitchen table writing, there is a moth on my bay window flapping its wings fervently, trying to break outside to the light. What is it about moths and their attraction to light? It reminds me of a story about a guy who thought he was a moth. One day he walked into a dentist's office and asked the receptionist if he could see the dentist about an emergency. She went to check; then told the man he could come back to see the dentist.

The man said to the dentist, "Doctor, you need to help me. I think I'm a moth."

The dentist replied, "I'm sorry, but I don't think I can help you. You need a psychiatrist."

The man replied, "I know that already."

---

10 Albert Barnes Notes on the Bible

"So why did you come to see me?" the dentist inquired.

To which the man replied, "Your light was on."

Light has the power to attract people. When we as believers live our lives "in the light" and "as a light" to the world, there is something remarkably attractive about us. But what does it mean to live in the light and as the light? Before I attempt to answer that question, give me a moment to do my good deed of the day and let this moth outside.

> *LIGHT HAS THE POWER TO ATTRACT PEOPLE. WHEN WE AS BELIEVERS LIVE OUR LIVES "IN THE LIGHT" AND "AS A LIGHT" TO THE WORLD, THERE IS SOMETHING REMARKABLY ATTRACTIVE ABOUT US.*

Okay, I'm back. And I feel much better about myself. I did my good deed for the day. So what does it mean to live in the light and as a light in this world? Here are a few thoughts that I hope will guide you to the light.

First, darkness in the Bible is synonymous with evil. In contrast, light is reflective of purity and doing the right thing. To be a light to the world means to live in a way that would not embarrass or shame you if shown on the five o'clock news. Light has varying degrees of brightness. Therefore, it is not just a matter of living a life that cannot be put to shame, but also shining with increasing brightness by living a life of personal integrity and accountability.

Another primary purpose of light is to help people see where they are going. A flashlight, night light, and street light are all intended to help us see where we are going. Then of course there is the amazing power of strobe lights. Strobe lights have the ability to make good dancers look super cool and bad dancers look all the funnier to watch. In either case, even a strobe light affects how we see the world.

> *WHEN GOD SHINES HIS LIGHT THROUGH YOU, PEOPLE SEE A UNIQUE COLOR BLEND OF YOUR GOD-GIVEN GIFTS, PERSONALITY, AND TALENTS IN ACTION.*

Speaking of strobe lights, light also has the ability to display color. If you come to a traffic light, you will see a red light, yellow light, or green light. To be a light in this world in one sense means being a colorful representations of God's character. Like a stained-glass window, our lives allow God's pure light to show the world many different colors. When God shines his light through you, people see a unique color blend of your God-given gifts, personality, and talents in action.

I took my kids the other day to Rita's Italian Ice, a Pennsylvania based frozen desserts franchise. If you have never enjoyed Rita's water ice, let me say that you have not yet lived! Water ice is somewhat like a snow cone, but with a more concentrated and saturated flavor. The young girl behind the counter was excited to give me a small sample of two new flavors—watermelon and coconut. She served them in tiny cups so I was able to try each flavor. After my taste test, the verdict is clear. Watermelon is amazing, and coconut is only for coconut lovers!

When Jesus said we are the light of the world, he was calling us to reflect his pure light to the people around us. Jesus is the true light, and when he shines through each of us, much like my analogy of the stained-glass window, other people can see a portion of that light, our own unique "flavor", you might say, like the watermelon and coconut flavored water ice. As people experience the good we do in the world, they are tasting the goodness of God for themselves. They are getting a sample, if you will, of God.

AS LOVERS OF GOOD FATHER, WE CANNOT KEEP THE GOODNESS OF GOD TO OURSELVES.

Jesus is adamant that we not hide the light he has given us. He makes this clear in the passage we just examined: "A city that is set on a hill cannot be hidden. Nor do they light a lamp and put it under a basket, but on a lampstand, and it gives light to all who are in the house."

Light cannot serve its purpose when hidden. It is only useful when displayed for all to see. As lovers of Our Good Father, we cannot keep the goodness of God to ourselves. We must be bold, step out of our comfort zones, and let our light shine in this world.

SALT, LIGHT, AND THE GLORY OF GOD

You may be asking yourself the question: "What does being salt and light have to do with the message of Our Good Father?"

The answer to this question is not only the main point of Jesus' message in the above passage, but the main take-away of this book.

It's the answer to the question I posed at the start of this chapter: "So now what?"

As we revel in the goodness of God the Father, painted clearly through the words of Jesus, we don't just receive the power of God's love, grace, and goodness for ourselves. We receive that same power, grace, love, and goodness to give away to others. The purpose of giving God's goodness away to the world is so that other people will desire to worship the Father as we do. That's what it means to do our good works so that others will glorify the Father.

Our kindness displayed in this world will attract people to want to worship God for themselves. Our salt is intended to make their lives taste better, to help them be made whole and hunger for more. Our light is meant to help people see truth more clearly so they will eventually choose to walk on the well-lit, but narrow path as Christ followers.

> *THE PURPOSE OF GIVING GOD'S GOODNESS AWAY TO THE WORLD IS SO THAT OTHER PEOPLE WILL DESIRE TO WORSHIP THE FATHER AS WE DO.*

The reason each of us chooses to submit our lives to God and Christ comes down to the fact that at some point in our journey we have recognized that God offers us something tangibly better than the world's schemes and system. We became convinced that we need God, not that he needs us, and we came to him on the basis of what he can do on our behalf—forgive our sins, give us hope, break our habits, cure our loneliness, turn our relationships around, give us purpose, save our souls. The list goes on. God is so good!

The apostle Paul explained how the goodness of God works in our lives this way:

Don't you see how wonderfully kind, tolerant, and patient God is with you? Does this mean nothing to you? Can't you see that his kindness is intended to turn you from your sin?[11]

Our goodness displayed in the world is meant to turn people from their sinful lives and redirect them instead to trust in a Savior who loved them unto death. Does that ship turn around overnight? Not always! For some people, coming to acceptance of God's goodness and Christ's sacrifice is relatively easy. With others, it may take years

---

11 Romans 2:4, New Living Translation

of sharing the goodness of God, both in word and action, along with a hailstorm of prayer before they even considering giving God a chance. At either extreme or anywhere in between, our own role as Christ followers does not change. We are to shine brightly and not lose our saltiness, knowing that our lives and good deeds have power to persuade and draw men to God.

THE FINISHED PRODUCT

At the start of this journey, we recognized that we ourselves may have come to this topic with a lot of blotches on our canvas. Hopefully after giving Jesus a blank canvas, we have now seen with our own eyes the beauty of God the Father as revealed through the words of Christ. And as those who have benefited from God's extravagant goodness, it is now our obligation to give his goodness away to the curious, skeptical, doubtful, and even hostile people around us.

We are God's workers, his tools, his resources, his team, and, above all, his beloved children who have been chosen and commissioned to share the message and blessing of God with others. Jesus said we do so by performing "good works" or deeds through which we can make the world scratch its head and wonder, "What's up with these people?"

Think of the guy who wrote the spiteful editorial to my local paper. He's not just an angry, upset, and hostile sinner. He's a lost son meandering through this world, grasping for something true and meaningful and right to live for and to fill the void in his life. While at this moment he cannot fully accept the beliefs of Christians, he can accept our good deeds done in love. People can refute our theology as long as they like, but they have a hard time challenging our good deeds. Consider this interaction between Jesus and the Jews of his day:

> [Jesus said] "I and My Father are one." Then the Jews took up stones again to stone him. Jesus answered them, "Many good works I have shown you from my father. For which of those works do you stone me?" The Jews answered him, saying, "For a good work we do not stone you, but for blasphemy, and because you, being a man, make yourself God."[12]

Did you hear that? "For a good work we do not stone you." Some

---

12 John 10:30-33, NKJV

people may never be convinced of our beliefs. Like the Jews who took up stones to throw at Jesus, they may write or speak hurtful words about us, our beliefs, and even our Savior. Despite this, the good deeds we perform in the Father's name will paint for them an irresistible, beautiful picture they cannot help but admire. As the apostle Paul described: "For we are God's handiwork, created in Christ Jesus to do good works, which God prepared in advance for us to do."[13]

Jesus' words to his original disciples apply equally to us today, "Peace be to you. As the Father has sent me, even so I send you."[14] So let's be artists who paint an irresistible picture of God the Father through our words, deeds, and ever increasing saltiness and brightness. Let's make the world wonder, "What's up with those God loving people anyway? They always go about doing good works and helping others!"

And when they ask us our story, we can tell them with unashamed conviction and grace, "Our Father is good!"

To Our Good Father be all the glory, honor and praise, Amen!

Points to Remember:
- People who do not accept and embrace what we believe may still receive our good deeds.
- Our good deeds function as salt, making our world tasteful and preserved.
- Our good deeds provide light for unbelievers to see the ways of God and know his goodness.

Prayer:
"Good Father, empower me to live out the good works that will help draw people closer to You."

Meditation:
Our good works glorify Our Good Father.

---

13 Ephesians 2:10, NIV
14 John 20:21

Group Discussion:

- How have the good works of Christians made an impact on your own faith?
- How do incongruities between a person's expressed belief and their actions affect you?
- Have you seen a time when your good deeds opened a person's heart up to God? If so, share.
- How can doing good deeds to help other people potentially strengthen your own faith in God?

Dig Deeper:

Read through the following verses to study more about our good works done for God.

- James 2:14-19: What good is it, my brothers and sisters, if someone claims to have faith but has no deeds? Can such faith save them? Suppose a brother or a sister is without clothes and daily food. If one of you says to them, "Go in peace; keep warm and well fed," but does nothing about their physical needs, what good is it? In the same way, faith by itself, if it is not accompanied by action, is dead. But someone will say, "You have faith; I have deeds." Show me your faith without deeds, and I will show you my faith by my deeds. You believe that there is one God. Good! Even the demons believe that—and shudder.
- Matthew 5:13-16: You are the salt of the earth; but if the salt loses its flavor, how shall it be seasoned? It is then good for nothing but to be thrown out and trampled underfoot by men. You are the light of the world. A city that is set on a hill cannot be hidden. Nor do they light a lamp and put it under a basket, but on a lampstand, and it gives light to all who are in the house. Let your light so shine before men, that they may see your good works and glorify your Father in heaven.
- Proverbs 31:8-9: Speak up for those who cannot speak for themselves, for the rights of all who are destitute. Speak up and judge fairly; defend the rights of the poor and needy.

Epilogue

A FINISHED PAINTING

"The reward of a thing well done is having done it."

- RALPH WALDO EMERSON

When I was in elementary school, I loved school art shows. I would work long and hard on a painting, drawing, or sculpture in art class. Then the day would come when my work was displayed in the school for all to see. My parents would show up, look at what I had created, and tell me just how proud they were of me.

Similarly, Jesus came to earth to paint a beautiful picture *of* the Father and a beautiful picture *for* the Father. And when the Father looked upon the painting of Jesus' life, he said, "This is my Son in whom I am well pleased."

At the beginning of our journey together through the pages of this book, I promised you that Jesus would paint a marvelous picture of the Father. And I hope you will now agree he has done just that. Jesus has painted a picture for us of a Father who provides for his children. The Father loves to meet the needs of his kids and wants us to trust him for provision.

Jesus painted a picture of a Father who rewards. Our Father does not take our work in his named for granted. Instead, he seeks to reward us for our labor, both in this world and the one to come. He loves when we do things without fanfare not for our own name's sake, but in the secrecy of our intimate relationship with him.

Jesus painted a picture of a Father who welcomes us home. He showed us that God is not standing angrily at the door with his arms closed and folded across his chest. He's not even standing at the door with his arms spread wide open. No, he's running down the road toward us as we approach his home. We are welcome to be home with God!

Jesus painted a picture of how we are to pray in reverence, but also in closeness to the Father. He taught us to pray outside of ourselves and with a view that encompasses the entire family of God in the picture. Jesus taught us to recognize the evil in this world, but also to pray for the Father's kingdom to rule and reign here on earth. Jesus painted a picture of a Father who guides our life. The Father desires us to ask him for great things in prayer and he loves to give in return. The Father wants us to seek his will diligently knowing he will guide our path. The Father wants us to boldly walk through the doors of opportunity set before us. The Father's will is always good and better than our own plans.

Jesus painted a picture of a Father who knows how to bless and do good even to unbelievers. The Father is universally good to all mankind, regardless of their ethnicity, social status, religious background, gender or sexual orientation. Father is an equal-opportunity provider of air, breath, life, health, and everything that is good. Father loves all of his creation and as his children we are called to do the same indiscriminately.

Jesus painted a picture of the father of lies, so we would be aware of the schemes and lies of the one who would try to distract us from our real Daddy. Our Father is not out to hurt us, harm us, shame us, or cause us more pain. He is out to heal, restore, make whole, and bring salvation to all mankind. Our Father is always good even when life seems unfair or unpleasant.

Jesus painted a picture of a Father who is trustworthy at all times. Even in the midst of our deepest and darkest moments, Jesus taught us that we can pray, "Loving Daddy". We know that God is writing a sequel to our story and is working a plan of redemption for our lives.

Our Father has not abandoned us. He will come through in our lives and be found faithful.

Jesus painted a picture of a Father who heals us. Our Good Father desires to bring healing to our emotions as much as he does salvation to our souls. It is when we forgive others, as Jesus did on the cross, that we experience the healing grace and power of Our Good Father. We need to remember Jesus words on the cross, "Father, forgive them" and make them our own.

Jesus painted a picture of a Father who accepts us right where we are in this life. In Christ we know that the Father has already accepted and approved of us. We learned that it is the Father's love for us that makes us whole, not our accomplishments. Our Good Father sees us as his beloved children, not as wretched sinners because of the work of Jesus on the cross.

Jesus painted a picture of a Father who wants to bring more children back to his home. He wants to use us, his children to do it. Father desires that our good works, life, and conduct become an attraction to the world around us. Father wants us to provide light to a dark world and salt to a tasteless world. We are to give the world a taste of what Our Good Father is really like.

AN UNFINISHED PAINTING

One of my best works of art in school was from an assignment our art teacher gave us to paint what our future would look like. I had this great idea of drawing circles that would represent phases of my life from birth to death. Within each circle I first drew the major events I foresaw taking place in my life—high school, college, marriage, kids, career etc. It was an awesome painting! The only problem was that I never finished my work. I ran out of time, and so to this day the painting is unfinished.

Now that you have reached the end of this book, you are probably thinking that the painting I promised you is finished. And for now, my part of the painting has come to a close. But the reality is that Jesus painted so much more than I was able to capture in these pages. The words you have read are only a dab of paint in the greater canvas of who Our Good Father is and what he is about.

So, my challenge to you is simply this: Don't stop exploring! The words of Jesus regarding the Father are so plentiful and robust that you could never exhaust them. Jesus has more beautiful pictures of the Father to paint. We only need to pick up the paintbrush of his Word and read.

To help you in that process, I have included as a resource a list of the words Jesus spoke about the Father (see Father References). You can take these scripture passages and do a few things with them to enhance your growth and relationship with the Father:

- Read them through slowly.
- Study them with friends.
- Meditate on them and ask God for understanding.
- Memorize the ones that are most significant to you.
- Make connections between different passages.
- Share them with friends who need to know the Father.
- Post your own thoughts, scriptures or memes on social media using hashtag #ourgoodfather.
- Visit www.ourgoodfather.com for free articles, social media and resources to share.

As we close our time together, I would like to offer a prayer for you. I have written it in the first person so you can pray it for yourself:

Good Father, I thank you for sending Jesus to paint this picture of you. Jesus, thank you for the way you have revealed the Father to me. Holy Spirit, continue to help me grow in my knowledge and understanding of Our Good Father. Teach, train, and guide me in my understanding of the person of God the Father. Loving Daddy, empower me this day and forever to live in such a way that helps people to know that you are truly good! Amen.

FATHER REFERENCES[1]

Even so, let your light shine before men; that they may see your good works, and glorify your **Father** who is in heaven. **(Matthew 5:16)**

that you may be children of your **Father** who is in heaven. For he makes his sun to rise on the evil and the good, and sends rain on the just and the unjust. **(Matthew 5:45)**

Therefore, you shall be perfect, just as your **Father** in heaven is perfect. **(Matthew 5:48)**

Be careful that you don't do your charitable giving before men, to be seen by them, or else you have no reward from your **Father** who is in heaven. **(Matthew 6:1)**

so that your merciful deeds may be in secret, then your **Father** who sees in secret will reward you openly. **(Matthew 6:4)**

But you, when you pray, enter into your inner chamber, and having shut your door, pray to your **Father** who is in secret, and your **Father** who sees in secret will reward you openly. **(Matthew 6:6)**

Therefore don't be like them, for your **Father** knows what things you need, before you ask him. **(Matthew 6:8)**

Pray like this: 'Our **Father** in heaven, may your name be kept holy.' **(Matthew 6:9)**

For if you forgive men their trespasses, your heavenly **Father** will also forgive you. **(Matthew 6:14)**

---

1   All of the scriptures in this section were taken from the World English Bible.

But if you don't forgive men their trespasses, neither will your **Father** forgive your trespasses. **(Matthew 6:15)**

so that you are not seen by men to be fasting, but by your **Father** who is in secret, and your **Father**, who sees in secret, will reward you. **(Matthew 6:18)**

See the birds of the sky, that they don't sow, neither do they reap, nor gather into barns. Your heavenly **Father** feeds them. Aren't you of much more value than they? **(Matthew 6:26)**

For the Gentiles seek after all these things, for your heavenly **Father** knows that you need all these things. **(Matthew 6:32)**

If you then, being evil, know how to give good gifts to your children, how much more will your **Father** who is in heaven give good things to those who ask him! **(Matthew 7:11)**

Not everyone who says to me, 'Lord, Lord,' will enter into the Kingdom of Heaven; but he who does the will of my **Father** who is in heaven. **(Matthew 7:21)**

For it is not you who speak, but the Spirit of your **Father** who speaks in you. **(Matthew 10:20)**

Aren't two sparrows sold for [a penny]? Not one of them falls on the ground apart from your **Father**'s will, **(Matthew 10:29)**

Everyone therefore who confesses me before men, him I will also confess before my **Father** who is in heaven. **(Matthew 10:32)**

But whoever denies me before men, him I will also deny before my **Father** who is in heaven. **(Matthew 10:33)**

At that time, Jesus answered, "I thank you, **Father**, Lord of heaven and earth, that you hid these things from the wise and understanding, and revealed them to infants. **(Matthew 11:25)**

Yes, **Father**, for so it was well-pleasing in your sight. **(Matthew 11:26)**

All things have been delivered to me by my **Father**. No one knows the Son, except the **Father**; neither does anyone know the **Father**, except the Son, and he to whom the Son desires to reveal him. **(Matthew 11:27)**

For whoever does the will of my **Father** who is in heaven, he is my brother, and sister, and mother. **(Matthew 12:50)**

Then the righteous will shine forth like the sun in the Kingdom of their **Father**. He who has ears to hear, let him hear. **(Matthew 13:43)**

But he answered, "Every plant which my heavenly **Father** didn't plant will be uprooted." **(Matthew 15:13)**

Jesus answered him, "Blessed are you, Simon Bar Jonah, for flesh and blood has not revealed this to you, but my **Father** who is in heaven." **(Matthew 16:17)**

For the Son of Man will come in the glory of his **Father** with his angels, and then he will render to everyone according to his deeds. **(Matthew 16:27)**

See that you don't despise one of these little ones, for I tell you that in heaven their angels always see the face of my **Father** who is in heaven. **(Matthew 18:10)**

Even so it is not the will of your **Father** who is in heaven that one of these little ones should perish. **(Matthew 18:14)**

Again, assuredly I tell you, that if two of you will agree on earth concerning anything that they will ask, it will be done for them by my **Father** who is in heaven. **(Matthew 18:19)**

So my heavenly **Father** will also do to you, if you don't each forgive your brother from your hearts for his misdeeds." **(Matthew 18:35)**

He said to them, "You will indeed drink my cup, and be baptized with the baptism that I am baptized with, but to sit on my right hand and on my left hand is not mine to give; but it is for whom it has been prepared by my **Father**." **(Matthew 20:23)**

Call no man on the earth your **Father**, for one is your **Father**, he who is in heaven. **(Matthew 23:9)**

But no one knows of that day and hour, not even the angels of heaven, but my **Father** only. **(Matthew 24:36)**

Then the King will tell those on his right hand, 'Come, blessed of my **Father**, inherit the Kingdom prepared for you from the foundation of the world;' **(Matthew 25:34)**

But I tell you that I will not drink of this fruit of the vine from now on, until that day when I drink it anew with you in my **Father**'s Kingdom. **(Matthew 26:29)**

He went forward a little, fell on his face, and prayed, saying, "My **Father**, if it is possible, let this cup pass away from me; nevertheless, not what I desire, but what you desire." **(Matthew 26:39)**

Again, a second time he went away, and prayed, saying, "My **Father**, if this cup can't pass away from me unless I drink it, your desire be done." **(Matthew 26:42)**

Or do you think that I couldn't ask my **Father**, and he would even now send me more than twelve legions of angels? **(Matthew 26:53)**

Therefore go, and make disciples of all nations, baptizing them in the name of the **Father** and of the Son and of the Holy Spirit, **(Matthew 28:19)**

For whoever will be ashamed of me and of my words in this adulterous and sinful generation, the Son of Man also will be ashamed of him, when he comes in the glory of his **Father** with the holy angels. **(Mark 8:38)**

Whenever you stand praying, forgive, if you have anything against anyone; so that your **Father**, who is in heaven, may also forgive you your transgressions. **(Mark 11:25)**

But if you do not forgive, neither will your **Father** in heaven forgive your transgressions. **(Mark 11:26)**

But of that day or that hour no one knows, not even the angels in heaven, nor the Son, but only the **Father**. **(Mark 13:32)**

He said, "Abba, **Father**, all things are possible to you. Please remove this cup from me. However, not what I desire, but what you desire." **(Mark 14:36)**

He said to them, "Why were you looking for me? Didn't you know that I must be in my **Father**'s house?" **(Luke 2:49)**

Therefore be merciful, Even as your **Father** is also merciful. **(Luke 6:36)**

For whoever will be ashamed of me and of my words, of him will the Son of Man be ashamed, when he comes in his glory, and the glory of the **Father**, and of the holy angels. **(Luke 9:26)**

In that same hour Jesus rejoiced in the Holy Spirit, and said, "I thank you, O **Father**, Lord of heaven and earth, that you have hidden these things from the wise and understanding, and revealed them to little children. Yes, **Father**, for so it was well-pleasing in your sight." **(Luke 10:21)**

Turning to the disciples, he said, "All things have been delivered to me by my **Father**. No one knows who the Son is, except the **Father**, and who the **Father** is, except the Son, and he to whomever the Son desires to reveal him." **(Luke 10:22)**

He said to them, "When you pray, say, 'Our **Father** in heaven, May your name be kept holy. May your Kingdom come. May your will be done on Earth, as it is in heaven." **(Luke 11:2)**

If you then, being evil, know how to give good gifts to your children, how much more will your heavenly **Father** give the Holy Spirit to those who ask him? **(Luke 11:13)**

For the nations of the world seek after all of these things, but your **Father** knows that you need these things. **(Luke 12:30)**

Don't be afraid, little flock, for it is your **Father**'s good pleasure to give you the Kingdom. **(Luke 12:32)**

The younger of them said to his **Father**, '**Father**, give me my share of your property.' He divided his livelihood between them. **(Luke 15:12)**

I will get up and go to my **Father**, and will tell him, "**Father**, I have sinned against heaven, and in your sight." **(Luke 15:18)**

The son said to him, '**Father**, I have sinned against heaven, and in your sight. I am no longer worthy to be called your son.' **(Luke 15:21)**

I confer on you a kingdom, even as my **Father** conferred on me, **(Luke 22:29)**

saying, "**Father**, if you are willing, remove this cup from me. Nevertheless, not my will, but yours, be done." **(Luke 22:42)**

Jesus said, "**Father**, forgive them, for they don't know what they are doing." Dividing his garments among them, they cast lots. **(Luke 23:34)**

Jesus, crying with a loud voice, said, "**Father**, into your hands I commit my spirit!" Having said this, he breathed his last. **(Luke 23:46)**

Behold, I send forth the promise of my **Father** on you. But wait in the city of Jerusalem until you are clothed with power from on high. **(Luke 24:49)**

The Word became flesh, and lived among us. We saw his glory, such glory as of the one and only Son of the **Father**, full of grace and truth. **(John 1:14)**

No one has seen God at any time. The one and only Son, who is in the bosom of the **Father**, he has declared him. **(John 1:18)**

To those who sold the doves, he said, "Take these things out of here! Don't make my **Father**'s house a marketplace!" **(John 2:16)**

The **Father** loves the Son, and has given all things into his hand. **(John 3:35)**

Jesus said to her, "Woman, believe me, the hour comes, when neither in this mountain, nor in Jerusalem, will you worship the **Father**." **(John 4:21)**

But the hour comes, and now is, when the true worshippers will worship the **Father** in spirit and truth, for the **Father** seeks such to be his worshippers. **(John 4:23)**

But Jesus answered them, "My **Father** is still working, so I am working, too." **(John 5:17)**

For this cause therefore the Jews sought all the more to kill him, because he not only broke the Sabbath, but also called God his own **Father**, making himself equal with God. **(John 5:18)**

Jesus therefore answered them, "Most assuredly, I tell you, the Son can do nothing of himself, but what he sees the **Father** doing. For whatever things he does, these the Son also does likewise." **(John 5:19)**

For the **Father** has affection for the Son, and shows him all things that he himself does. He will show him greater works than these, that you may marvel. **(John 5:20)**

For as the **Father** raises the dead and gives them life, even so the Son also gives life to whom he desires. **(John 5:21)**

For the **Father** judges no one, but he has given all judgment to the Son, **(John 5:22)**

that all may honor the Son, even as they honor the **Father**. He who doesn't honor the Son doesn't honor the **Father** who sent him. **(John 5:23)**

For as the **Father** has life in himself, even so he gave to the Son also to have life in himself. **(John 5:26)**

I can of myself do nothing. As I hear, I judge, and my judgment is righteous; because I don't seek my own will, but the will of my **Father** who sent me. **(John 5:30)**

But the testimony which I have is greater than that of John, for the works which the **Father** gave me to accomplish, the very works that I do, testify about me, that the **Father** has sent me. **(John 5:36)**

The **Father** himself, who sent me, has testified about me. You have neither heard his voice at any time, nor seen his form. **(John 5:37)**

I have come in my **Father**'s name, and you don't receive me. If another comes in his own name, you will receive him. **(John 5:43)**

Don't think that I will accuse you to the **Father**. There is one who accuses you, even Moses, on whom you have set your hope. **(John 5:45)**

Don't work for the food which perishes, but for the food which remains to eternal life, which the Son of Man will give to you. For God the **Father** has sealed him. **(John 6:27)**

Jesus therefore said to them, "Most assuredly, I tell you, it wasn't Moses who gave you the bread out of heaven, but my **Father** gives you the true bread out of heaven." **(John 6:32)**

All those who the **Father** gives me will come to me. Him who comes to me I will in no way throw out. **(John 6:37)**

This is the will of my **Father** who sent me, that of all he has given to me I should lose nothing, but should raise him up at the last day. **(John 6:39)**

No one can come to me unless the **Father** who sent me draws him, and I will raise him up in the last day. **(John 6:44)**

It is written in the prophets, 'They will all be taught by God.' Therefore everyone who hears from the **Father**, and has learned, comes to me. **(John 6:45)**

Not that anyone has seen the **Father**, except he who is from God. He has seen the **Father**. **(John 6:46)**

As the living **Father** sent me, and I live because of the **Father**; so he who feeds on me, he will also live because of me. **(John 6:57)**

He said, "For this cause have I said to you that no one can come to me, unless it is given to him by my **Father**." **(John 6:65)**

Even if I do judge, my judgment is true, for I am not alone, but I am with the **Father** who sent me. **(John 8:16)**

I am one who testifies about myself, and the **Father** who sent me testifies about me. **(John 8:18)**

They said therefore to him, "Where is your **Father**?" Jesus answered, "You know neither me, nor my **Father**. If you knew me, you would know my **Father** also." **(John 8:19)**

They didn't understand that he spoke to them about the **Father**. **(John 8:27)**

Jesus therefore said to them, "When you have lifted up the Son of Man, then you will know that I AM he, and I do nothing of myself, but as my **Father** taught me, I say these things."**(John 8:28)**

He who sent me is with me. The **Father** hasn't left me alone, for I always do the things that are pleasing to him. **(John 8:29)**

I say the things which I have seen with my **Father**; and you also do the things which you have seen with your **Father**. **(John 8:38)**

You do the works of your **Father**. They said to him, "We were not born of sexual immorality. We have one **Father**, God." **(John 8:41)**

Therefore Jesus said to them, "If God were your **Father**, you would love me, for I came out and have come from God. For I haven't come of myself, but he sent me." **(John 8:42)**

Jesus answered, "I don't have a demon, but I honor my **Father**, and you dishonor me." **(John 8:49)**

Jesus answered, "If I glorify myself, my glory is nothing. It is my **Father** who glorifies me, of whom you say that he is our God." **(John 8:54)**

even as the **Father** knows me, and I know the **Father**. I lay down my life for the sheep. **(John 10:15)**

Therefore the **Father** loves me, because I lay down my life, that I may take it again. **(John 10:17)**

No one takes it away from me, but I lay it down by myself. I have power to lay it down, and I have power to take it again. I received this commandment from my **Father**. **(John 10:18)**

Jesus answered them, "I told you, and you don't believe. The works that I do in my **Father**'s name, these testify about me." **(John 10:25)**

My **Father**, who has given them to me, is greater than all. No one is able to snatch them out of my **Father**'s hand. **(John 10:29)**

I and the **Father** are one. **(John 10:30)**

Jesus answered them, "I have shown you many good works from my **Father**. For which of those works do you stone me?" **(John 10:32)**

Do you say of him whom the **Father** sanctified and sent into the world, 'You blaspheme,' because I said, 'I am the Son of God? **(John 10:36)**

If I don't do the works of my **Father**, don't believe me. **(John 10:37)**

But if I do them, though you don't believe me, believe the works; that you may know and believe that the **Father** is in me, and I in the **Father**. **(John 10:38)**

So they took away the stone from the place where the dead man was lying. Jesus lifted up his eyes, and said, "**Father**, I thank you that you listen to me." **(John 11:41)**

If anyone serves me, let him follow me. Where I am, there will my servant also be. If anyone serves me, the **Father** will honor him. **(John 12:26)**

Now my soul is troubled. What shall I say? '**Father**, save me from this time?' But for this cause I came to this time. **(John 12:27)**

Father, glorify your name!" Then there came a voice out of the sky, saying, "I have both glorified it, and will glorify it again." **(John 12:28)**

For I spoke not from myself, but the **Father** who sent me, he gave me a commandment, what I should say, and what I should speak. **(John 12:49)**

I know that his commandment is eternal life. The things therefore which I speak, even as the **Father** has said to me, so I speak." **(John 12:50)**

Now before the feast of the Passover, Jesus, knowing that his time had come that he would depart from this world to the **Father**, having loved his own who were in the world, he loved them to the end. **(John 13:1)**

Jesus, knowing that the **Father** had given all things into his hands, and that he came forth from God, and was going to God, **(John 13:3)**

In my **Father**'s house are many mansions. If it weren't so, I would have told you. I am going to prepare a place for you. **(John 14:2)**

Jesus said to him, "I am the way, the truth, and the life. No one comes to the **Father**, except through me." **(John 14:6)**

If you had known me, you would have known my **Father** also. From now on, you know him, and have seen him. **(John 14:7)**

Philip said to him, "Lord, show us the **Father**, and that will be enough for us." **(John 14:8)**

Jesus said to him, "Have I been with you such a long time, and do you not know me, Philip? He who has seen me has seen the **Father**. How do you say, 'Show us the **Father**?'" **(John 14:9)**

Don't you believe that I am in the **Father**, and the **Father** in me? The words that I tell you, I speak not from myself; but the **Father** who lives in me does his works. **(John 14:10)**

Believe me that I am in the **Father**, and the **Father** in me; or else believe me for the very works' sake. **(John 14:11)**

Most assuredly I tell you, he who believes in me, the works that I do, he will do also; and he will do greater works than these, because I am going to my **Father**. **(John 14:12)**

Whatever you will ask in my name, that will I do, that the **Father** may be glorified in the Son. **(John 14:13)**

I will pray to the **Father**, and he will give you another Counselor, that he may be with you forever **(John 14:16)**

In that day you will know that I am in my **Father**, and you in me, and I in you. **(John 14:20)**

One who has my commandments, and keeps them, that person is one who loves me. One who loves me will be loved by my **Father**, and I will love him, and will reveal myself to him. **(John 14:21)**

Jesus answered him, "If a man loves me, he will keep my word. My **Father** will love him, and we will come to him, and make our home with him." (**John 14:23**)

He who doesn't love me doesn't keep my words. The word which you hear isn't mine, but the **Father**'s who sent me. (**John 14:24**)

But the Counselor, the Holy Spirit, whom the **Father** will send in my name, he will teach you all things, and will remind you of all that I said to you. (**John 14:26**)

You heard how I told you, 'I go away, and I come to you.' If you loved me, you would have rejoiced, because I said 'I am going to my **Father**;' for the **Father** is greater than I. (**John 14:28**)

But that the world may know that I love the **Father**, and as the **Father** commanded me, even so I do. Arise, let us go from here. (**John 14:31**)

I am the true vine, and my **Father** is the farmer. (**John 15:1**)

In this is my **Father** glorified, that you bear much fruit; and so you will be my disciples. (**John 15:8**)

Even as the **Father** has loved me, I also have loved you. Remain in my love. (**John 15:9**)

If you keep my commandments, you will remain in my love; even as I have kept my **Father**'s commandments, and remain in his love. (**John 15:10**)

No longer do I call you servants, for the servant doesn't know what his lord does. But I have called you friends, for everything that I heard from my **Father**, I have made known to you. (**John 15:15**)

You didn't choose me, but I chose you, and appointed you, that you should go and bear fruit, and that your fruit should remain; that whatever you will ask of the **Father** in my name, he may give it to you. (**John 15:16**)

He who hates me, hates my **Father** also. (**John 15:23**)

If I hadn't done among them the works which no one else did, they wouldn't have had sin. But now have they seen and also hated both me and my **Father**. (**John 15:24**)

When the Counselor has come, whom I will send to you from the **Father**, the Spirit of truth, who proceeds from the **Father**, he will testify about me. **(John 15:26)**

They will do these things because they have not known the **Father**, nor me. **(John 16:3)**

about righteousness, because I am going to my **Father**, and you won't see me anymore; **(John 16:10)**

All things whatever the **Father** has are mine; therefore I said that he takes of mine, and will declare it to you. **(John 16:15)**

Some of his disciples therefore said to one another, "What is this that he says to us, 'A little while, and you won't see me, and again a little while, and you will see me;' and, 'Because I go to the **Father**?'" **(John 16:17)**

In that day you will ask me no questions. Most assuredly I tell you, whatever you may ask of the **Father** in my name, he will give it to you. **(John 16:23)**

I have spoken these things to you in figures of speech. But the time is coming when I will no more speak to you in figures of speech, but will tell you plainly about the **Father**. **(John 16:25)**

In that day you will ask in my name; and I don't say to you, that I will pray to the **Father** for you, **(John 16:26)**

for the **Father** himself loves you, because you have loved me, and have believed that I came forth from God. **(John 16:27)**

I came out from the **Father**, and have come into the world. Again, I leave the world, and go to the **Father**. **(John 16:28)**

Behold, the time is coming, yes, and has now come, that you will be scattered, everyone to his own place, and you will leave me alone. Yet I am not alone, because the **Father** is with me. **(John 16:32)**

Jesus said these things, and lifting up his eyes to heaven, he said, "**Father**, the time has come. Glorify your Son, that your Son may also glorify you;" **(John 17:1)**

Now, **Father**, glorify me with your own self with the glory which I had with you before the world existed. **(John 17:5)**

I am no more in the world, but these are in the world, and I am coming to you. Holy **Father**, keep them through your name which you have given me, that they may be one, even as we are. **(John 17:11)**

that they may all be one; even as you, **Father**, are in me, and I in you, that they also may be one in us; that the world may believe that you sent me. **(John 17:21)**

Father, I desire that they also whom you have given me be with me where I am, that they may see my glory, which you have given me, for you loved me before the foundation of the world. **(John 17:24)**

Righteous **Father**, the world hasn't known you, but I know you; and these know that you sent me. **(John 17:25)**

Jesus therefore said to Peter, "Put the sword into its sheath. The cup which the **Father** has given me, shall I not surely drink it?" **(John 18:11)**

Jesus said to her, "Don't touch me, for I haven't yet ascended to my **Father**; but go to my brothers, and tell them, 'I am ascending to my **Father** and your **Father**, to my God and your God.'" **(John 20:17)**

Jesus therefore said to them again, "Peace be to you. As the **Father** has sent me, even so I send you." **(John 20:21)**

As an additional supplement, you will find The Father's Love Letter on the following two pages. This letter reveals the goodness of God the Father through both Old and New Testament passages.

FATHER'S LOVE LETTER

My Child,

You may not know me, but I know everything about you. PSALM 139:1 / I know when you sit down and when you rise up. PSALM 139:2 / I am familiar with all your ways. PSALM 139:3 / Even the very hairs on your head are numbered. MATTHEW 10:29-31 / For you were made in my image. GENESIS 1:27 / In me you live and move and have your being. ACTS 17:28 / For you are my offspring. ACTS 17:28 / I knew you even before you were conceived. JEREMIAH 1:4-5 / I chose you when I planned creation. EPHESIANS 1:11-12 / You were not a mistake, for all your days are written in my book. PSALM 139:15-16 / I determined the exact time of your birth and where you would live. ACTS 17:26 / You are fearfully and wonderfully made. PSALM 139:14 / I knit you together in your mother's womb. PSALM 139:13 / And brought you forth on the day you were born. PSALM 71:6 / I have been misrepresented by those who don't know me. JOHN 8:41-44 / I am not distant and angry, but am the complete expression of love. 1 JOHN 4:16 / And it is my desire to lavish my love on you. 1 JOHN 3:1 / Simply because you are my child and I am your Father. 1 JOHN 3:1 / I offer you more than your earthly father ever could. MATTHEW 7:11 / For I am the perfect father. MATTHEW 5:48 / Every good gift that you receive comes from my hand. JAMES 1:17 / For I am your provider and I meet all your needs. MATTHEW 6:31-33 / My plan for your future has always been filled with hope. JEREMIAH 29:11 / Because I love you with an everlasting love. JEREMIAH 31:3 / My thoughts toward you are countless as the sand on the seashore. PSALM 139:17-18 / And I rejoice over you with singing. ZEPHANIAH 3:17 / I will never stop doing good to you. JEREMIAH 32:40 / For you are my treasured possession.

EXODUS 19:5 / I desire to establish you with all my heart and all my soul. JEREMIAH 32:41 / And I want to show you great and marvelous things. JEREMIAH 33:3 / If you seek me with all your heart, you will find me. DEUTERONOMY 4:29 / Delight in me and I will give you the desires of your heart. PSALM 37:4 / For it is I who gave you those desires. PHILIPPIANS 2:13 / I am able to do more for you than you could possibly imagine. EPHESIANS 3:20 / For I am your greatest encourager. 2 THESSALONIANS 2:16-17 / I am also the Father who comforts you in all your troubles. 2 CORINTHIANS 1:3-4 / When you are brokenhearted, I am close to you. PSALM 34:18 / As a shepherd carries a lamb, I have carried you close to my heart. ISAIAH 40:11 / One day I will wipe away every tear from your eyes. REVELATION 21:3-4 / And I'll take away all the pain you have suffered on this earth. REVELATION 21:3-4 / I am your Father, and I love you even as I love my son, Jesus. JOHN 17:23 / For in Jesus, my love for you is revealed. JOHN 17:26 / He is the exact representation of my being. HEBREWS 1:3 / He came to demonstrate that I am for you, not against you. ROMANS 8:31 / And to tell you that I am not counting your sins. 2 CORINTHIANS 5:18-19 / Jesus died so that you and I could be reconciled. 2 CORINTHIANS 5:18-19 / His death was the ultimate expression of my love for you. 1 JOHN 4:10 / I gave up everything I loved that I might gain your love. ROMANS 8:31-32 / If you receive the gift of my son Jesus, you receive me. 1 JOHN 2:23 / And nothing will ever separate you from my love again. ROMANS 8:38-39 / Come home and I'll throw the biggest party heaven has ever seen. LUKE 15:7 / I have always been Father, and will always be Father. EPHESIANS 3:14-15

My question is…Will you be my child? JOHN 1:12-13

I am waiting for you. LUKE 15:11-32

Love, Your Dad.

Almighty God

Father's Love Letter used by permission Father Heart Communications ©1999 FathersLoveLetter.com

About the Author

Pierre Eade is a pastor, author, speaker and coach whose mission is to inspire, educate and empower people to grow.

His first book, *Born to Grow*, is an entertaining exploration of the four pathways of growth God has for your life.

You can learn more about Pierre, read his blog, join his mailing list, connect with him on social media and contact him for speaking, writing or coaching by visiting: www.pierreeade.com.

For more information and resources on this book, please visit: www.ourgoodfather.com

ALSO AVAILABLE FROM PIERRE EADE

Pierre's first book, *Born to Grow*, is an entertaining exploration of the four pathways of growth God has for your life. In this book, you will...

- Understand how God works everything for your good.
- Discover God's ultimate goal for your life.
- Learn four distinct ways God wants you to grow.
- Be inspired, led and empowered by the Holy Spirit to become increasingly more like Jesus.

Take the exciting and joyful journey of growth with God!

"*Born to Grow* by Pierre Eade provides any Christian seeking to personally worship God in spirit and truth with a wonderful, practical guide for spiritual maturing in Christ.

– ROBERT STERNS, FOUNDER AND DIRECTOR OF EAGLES' WINGS

You must read Pierre Eade's, *Born to Grow*. His delightful humor, stories, insights, and growing tips will encourage, motivate, and empower you in the joyful journey of spiritual growth in Christ.

–DR. LARRY KEEFAUVER, BESTSELLING CHRISTIAN AUTHOR, INTERNATIONAL TEACHER

"Take the journey of spiritual growth from one of the churches' most promising young authors. *Born to Grow* is refreshing, insightful and inspiring! It is one of the most enjoyable books that I have read in a long time.

– DR. SCOTT MCDERMOTT, LEAD PASTOR, NEW TESTAMENT SCHOLAR, INTERNATIONAL SPEAKER